Disc
D1045645

Hinduism
A Beginner's Guide

Tenney Memorial Library
4886 Main Street South
P.O Box 85 Newbury, VT 05051
Phone: 802-866-5366

ONEWORLD BEGINNER'S GUIDES combine an original, inventive, and engaging approach with expert analysis on subjects ranging from art and history to religion and politics, and everything in-between. Innovative and affordable, books in the series are perfect for anyone curious about the way the world works and the big ideas of our time.

aesthetics
africa
american politics
anarchism
animal behaviour
anthropology
anti-capitalism
aquinas
archaeology
art
artificial intelligence
the baha'i faith
the beat generation
the bible
biodiversity
bioterror & biowarfare
the brain
british politics
the Buddha
cancer
censorship
christianity
civil liberties
classical music
climate change
cloning
the cold war
conservation
crimes against humanity
criminal psychology
critical thinking
the crusades
daoism
democracy
descartes
dewey
dyslexia
energy
engineering
the english civil wars
the enlightenment
epistemology
ethics
the european union
evolution
evolutionary psychology
existentialism
fair trade
feminism
forensic science
french literature
the french revolution
genetics
global terrorism
hinduism
history
the history of medicine
history of science
homer
humanism
huxley
international relations
iran
islamic philosophy
the islamic veil
journalism
judaism
lacan
life in the universe
literary theory
machiavelli
mafia & organized crime
magic
marx
medieval philosophy
the middle east
modern slavery
NATO
the new testament
nietzsche
nineteenth-century art
the northern ireland conflict
nutrition
oil
opera
the palestine–israeli conflict
particle physics
paul
philosophy
philosophy of mind
philosophy of religion
philosophy of science
planet earth
postmodernism
psychology
quantum physics
the qur'an
racism
rawls
reductionism
religion
renaissance art
the roman empire
the russian revolution
shakespeare
the small arms trade
sufism
the torah
the united nations
volcanoes
world war II
the world trade organization

Beginners GUIDES

Hinduism
A Beginner's Guide

Klaus K. Klostermaier

ONEWORLD

A Oneworld Book

First published by Oneworld Publications as *Hinduism, A Short Introduction*, 1998
Reissued 2000, reprinted 2002
First published in the *Beginners Guide* series, 2008
Reprinted 2010, 2012, 2015

Copyright © Klaus Klostermaier, 1998

All rights reserved
Copyright under Berne Convention
A CIP record for this title is available
from the British Library

ISBN 978-1-85168-538-7
eISBN 978-1-78074-026-3

Typeset by Jayvee, Trivandrum, India
Cover design by Two Associates
Printed and bound by Clays Ltd, St Ives plc
Ann Arbor, America

Oneworld Publications
10 Bloomsbury Street, London, WC1B 3SR, England
www.oneworld-publications.com

Stay up to date with the latest books,
special offers, and exclusive content from
Oneworld with our monthly newsletter

Sign up on our website
www.oneworld-publications.com

Contents

Preface

This beginner's guide to Hinduism is the first volume in a trilogy which includes *Hinduism: A Short History* and *Hindu Writings: A Short Introduction to the Major Sources.* The latter offers extracts from classical and modern sources paralleling and supporting the *Short Introduction.* It also contains a full bibliography of all literature referred to. The *Short History* provides a chronological overview of the development of Hinduism from its beginnings till now. *A Concise Encyclopedia of Hinduism* summarizes in a lexical form the information contained in the three volumes.

Hinduism: A Beginner's Guide does not presuppose any knowledge of the subject, nor does it aim to exhaust it. It is written for the interested general reader and hopes to generate further interest in this rich and vast culture. The reading list on page 4 suggests titles of a general nature that will help to broaden and deepen the information offered here. Short, specialized reading lists are given at the end of each chapter. I hope that readers will find this beginner's guide to Hinduism not only informative but also enjoyable.

There remains the pleasant duty of acknowledging help and support in preparing this book. I thank in particular my wife, Dr Doris Klostermaier, who carefully read the whole manuscript and made me aware of the need to give due attention to women's concerns in Hinduism. I thank Sonja Droege for checking the manuscript for spelling and grammar. I owe much to Dr Julius Lipner (Cambridge) who made numerous detailed suggestions for improvement. Last, but not least, I wish to thank Novin and Juliet

Doostdar and their staff from Oneworld for their interest and care in the production of this volume.

Klaus K. Klostermaier
Oxford

Note on pronunciation of Indian words and names

Many Indian names and Indian technical terms must be mentioned in describing Hinduism, and diacritics have been used to mark those sounds that do not have exact equivalents in English. Words that have become part of English vocabulary have not been provided with diacritics (e.g. Hindu instead of Hindū). Indian proper names have been reproduced as they are found in the sources. Indian words do not have accents: when a word contains long vowels, all of these receive a stress; otherwise the first syllable is stressed.

Vowels are spoken approximately like Italian vowels. A dash on top of an **ā**, **ī** and **ū** indicates a lengthening (doubling). **E**, **o**, **au** are always long.

There are many consonants in Indian languages that have no English equivalents. One of the peculiarities of Indian languages are aspirate consonants: **kh, gh, th, dh, ch, jh**. The 'h' in these is clearly pronounced as an aspirate. **Ś** and **ṣ** are pronounced 'sh'; c like 'ch' in chocolate; **j** like 'j' in 'jolly'. Sanskrit has a variety of 't' and 'd', as well as 'n', sounds, which have no equivalent in English. They are marked as (**ṭ**, **ḍ**, **ṇ**, **ṅ**, **ñ**. While not noticeable to someone unfamiliar with Indian languages, differences have to be indicated because word meanings change accordingly. **Ṛ** is pronounced 'ri'.

Words are given in their stem forms, i.e. without the inflections that indicate cases. Plurals of Indian words have been formed like English plurals, i.e. by simply adding an -s to the singular form (disregarding Sanskrit plural formations).

Maps

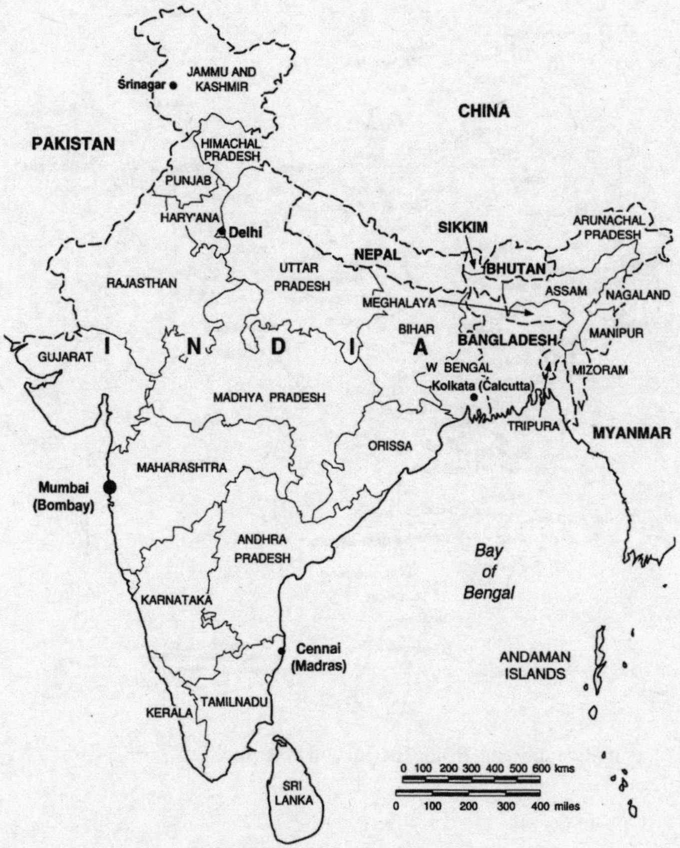

Map of India showing present state boundaries

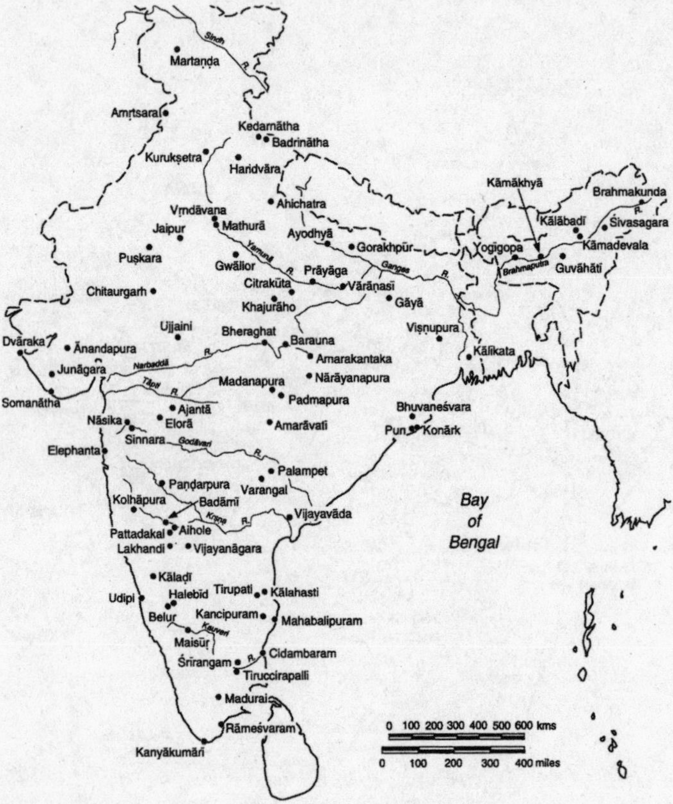

Map of India showing major ancient and holy places

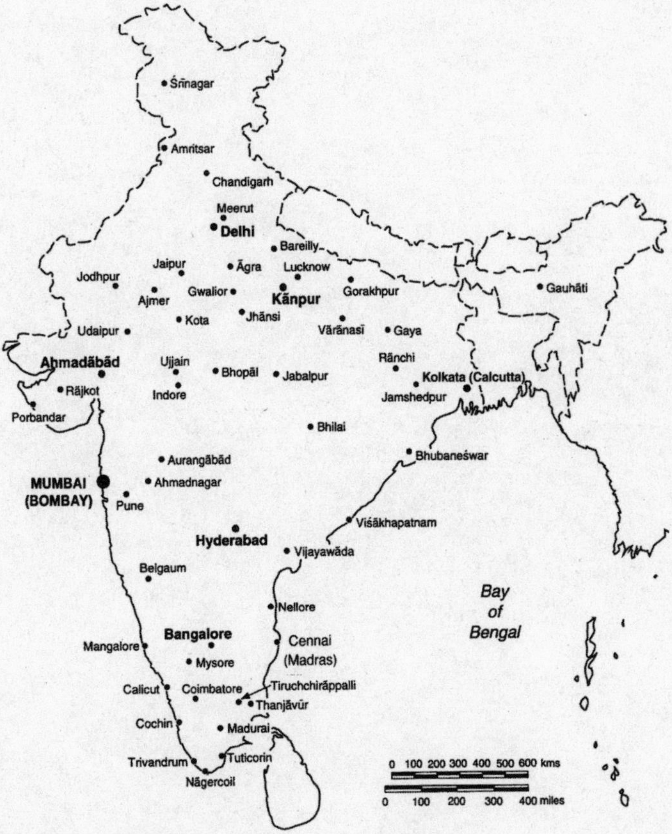

Map of India showing major modern urban centres

Introduction

Hinduism is:

- a pilgrimage to Tirupati
- a political programme
- a profound philosophy
- a way of life
- a sermon on the *Bhagavadgītā*
- a life of asceticism
- a joyful evening of hymn singing at a home in Bombay
- a ritual routine for Brahmins
- a temple festival at Madurai
- a dip in the Ganges

and many, many other things to the over eight hundred million people who are called Hindus.

Hinduism has no known founder and its beginnings point to pre-historic roots. It is unquestionably the oldest living major religious tradition. Until recently one could not become a Hindu – one had to be born a Hindu. Only someone belonging to a recognized *jātī* (caste), with a Hindu mother and father, who had undergone the prescribed rituals and had not committed a breach of the traditional way of life, could be a member of the Hindu community. Originally Hinduism was confined to India – crossing the dark sea, emigrating to the West, was associated with loss of caste and exclusion from the Hindu community. Nowadays there are an estimated forty-five million Hindus living outside India, of whom about eighteen million live in Nepal, the only country in the world which has declared Hinduism its state religion, and about fifteen million in Bangladesh, the former East Bengal; about two million Hindus live in Western Europe and North America; and modern Hindu missionary movements also attract westerners to their fold, granting them equal status with born Hindus.

Hinduism appears in a bewildering variety of shapes and forms and is presented and interpreted by its adherents in such a multitude of ways that it is extremely difficult to describe and impossible to define, as far as its content is concerned. While in the West it is treated as one of the major religions in the world, for Hindus it is much more than that: it is a way of life, a large and rich culture, an environment that envelops a Hindu from before birth to after death. What we call Hinduism, Hindus themselves designate as *sanātana dharma*, 'eternal law'. It is identical with universally valid and generally binding insights and precepts, specified so as to accord with individuals' standing within society. Within the framework of the *sanātana dharma* a great many different *saṁpradāyas*, religious communities with specific beliefs, rituals and places of worship, flourish.

Traditions that have histories of thousands of years, like Hinduism or Christianity, have branched out into many different phenotypes that are often in opposition to each other. Adherents of one of the existing branches often claim to be the only true representatives of tradition, accusing others of having betrayed or misinterpreted the original message. From such a sectarian standpoint it would be meaningless to attempt a global description of the tradition as a whole, and one would have to content oneself with a parallel treatment of major religious communities. However, what appears to the insider as essential difference is often seen by the outsider as but a variation on a theme that can be perceived and traced back to the origins. In a representation of Hinduism as a whole, as is attempted here, we will not overlook the major differences that brought the major and minor *saṁpradāyas* into existence and make them the communities they are. We will, however, aim not to lose the larger perspectives, and emphasize common origins as well as common themes that tie the hundreds of different manifestations of Hinduism together. That makes it meaningful to speak of 'Hinduism' instead of juxtaposing detailed descriptions of hundreds of unrelated communities that each have their own peculiar beliefs and practices.

In this beginner's guide we shall deal with four approaches designed to throw light on various dimensions of Hinduism:

1. the cultural-sociological framework provided by the Vedic tradition to which all Hindus subscribe, at least nominally
2. the great diversity of religions, such as Vaiṣṇavism, Śaivism, Śāktism and their subdivisions, which separates Hindus into many different and sometimes competitive communities
3. the intense intellectual quest that led to the development of numerous philosophical schools concerned with universal issues
4. the developments within Hinduism triggered off by its encounter with the modern West since the late eighteenth century.

As one would expect, there is a wide spread of individual commitment and active practice of religion among Hindus. There are those who devote their entire lives to practising and propagating a particular devotion or philosophy, and there are others for whom Hinduism is an embarrassment, a remnant from an unenlightened age, a formality that one submits to for the sake of family. As a community, however, Hindus are arguably the most intensely religious people on earth. Nowhere but in India can one find such enormous masses participating in religious festivities, and nowhere else can one find so many temples, shrines and images that attract constant worshippers. Hinduism as a culture has also become highly relevant in Indian politics in recent decades. Political parties utilize traditional symbols and popular practices to attract people's attention and to promote Hindu agenda.

This beginner's guide cannot aspire to an exhaustive description of even a small part of Hindu reality. What it attempts to do is to highlight important expressions of the Hindu tradition in such a way that Hindus can recognize it as their own and non-Hindus can understand some of the aspects of living Hinduism. The emphasis will be on the 'ideal' that Hinduism aims at, not on the empirical and historical 'facts'. Religions mean to provide their followers with notions of human perfection and ideals of life; shortcomings of adherents of a particular religion, however evident and gross, must not be blamed on the tradition or identified with it.

For thousands of years India has been a veritable laboratory of religion: everything imaginable seems to have been tried out, and nothing ever completely rejected. Homegrown religions and religions from outside have existed side by side, mostly peacefully, sometimes in competition with each other, occasionally violently clashing. In spite of many attacks on Hinduism, from inside and outside, in spite of rumours of decay and disarray, Hinduism has outlived all announcements of its impending demise. It may appear amorphous and archaic but it has put its stamp on all religions that attempted to displace it.

Hinduism has been compared to a huge Banyan tree which keeps growing and developing ever new roots that transform into trunks, from which grow new shoots and branches, again and again. Hinduism is infinitely fascinating, surprising and challenging. Something of this fascination and challenge which the author experienced in his many years of life in India and in his many more years of studying and teaching Hinduism will hopefully become apparent in this *Beginner's Guide to Hinduism*.

Suggested further reading

Brockington, J. L. *The Sacred Thread. Hinduism in its Continuity and Diversity*. Edinburgh University Press: Edinburgh, 1981.

Fuller, C. J. *The Camphor Flame. Popular Hinduism and Society in India*. Princeton University Press: Princeton, 1992.

Klostermaier, Klaus K. *A Survey of Hinduism*, State University of New York Press: Albany, NJ, 2nd ed. 1994.
Lipner, Julius. *Hindus. Their religious beliefs and practices*. Routledge: London and New York, 1994.
Mittal, S. and Q. Thursby (eds). *The Hindu World*. Routledge: New York and London, 2004.
Radhakrishnan, Sarvepalli. *Indian Philosophy*. 2 vols. George Allen & Unwin: London. First published in 1927. Many reprints.

See also the short reading lists at the end of each chapter.

Part I
The Vedic Tradition

Before the words 'Hindu' and 'Hinduism' became accepted (they are terms introduced by foreigners – Persians, Greeks and the English) the Hindus called their tradition *vaidika dharma*, the vedic *dharma*. *Dharma* is one of those words that are virtually untranslatable because of the large number of meanings they have in their original context. It only partly overlaps with the Western notion of 'religion'. It designates first and foremost the universal law that is believed to govern everything and that existed even before the creation. In a more specific sense vedic *dharma* is the application of this universal, timeless law to Indian society and the regulation of all aspects of life according to its principles. Its most basic and socially relevant expression is the stratification of Indian society into four hierarchically ordered *varṇas* (literally 'colours').

Vedic *dharma* is built on the assumption that all humans have rights and duties according to the *varṇa* they are born into. Vedic *dharma* is based on a large mass of canonical literature, collectively called 'Veda (knowledge)'. It was transmitted orally for many centuries and kept secret from outsiders, and was commented upon and interpreted by respected scholars and sages whose work also acquired a status of authority. Veda-based notions of caste, vedic rituals accompanying birth, marriage and death, vedic notions of purity and pollution, and vedic divisions of life-stages provide a framework that still effectively shapes the collective and individual existence of Hindus. Other aspects of vedic *dharma*, such as the prominence of *yajñas* (sacrifices), the memorization and recitation of vedic texts and certain beliefs concerning life after death expressed in them, have become marginal and have largely been replaced by more 'modern' forms of worship and more recent teachings, as expressed in the epics and Purāṇas.

In this part we will explore the origins of Hinduism, focusing both on traditional Indian and scholarly Western points of view. We will provide a brief summary of the scriptural basis of vedic *dharma*, go into some detail on the division of society and life-stages, and give a description of the rituals associated with it.

While vedic religion in its own age and time was certainly a 'complete' tradition, it was overlaid in later times by Purāṇic Hinduism and by later philosophical and socio-political developments. But it was never abolished or replaced. It forms the basis of Hinduism and is still alive in present-day India. The real Hinduism of the Indian people is the accumulation of many different layers of religion. To consider one aspect only would be to miss out on Hinduism as such. There are scholars who criticize a philosophical system like Śaṇkara's *Advaita Vedānta* for its alleged lack of ethics. Leaving aside the question of an Advaita ethic for the time being, one should note that before beginning a study of Advaita, a Hindu would have been introduced to his tradition through a study of the *Dharmaśāstras* (lawbooks), which contain a very detailed and sophisticated ethic – an ethic which is binding also for a student of Advaita.

1

Origins of Hinduism

All are agreed that Hinduism has no known founder and that its origins go far back into the past; much further than those of any other living major religion. Similarly, there is no doubt that what is called Hinduism today is the result of many developments, the fusion and fission of diverse religious movements. The result of these processes is a 'religion' that exhibits the most diverse and contradictory features. Hinduism is often called a 'family of religions' rather than one religion, and even within this 'family' the differences are often more pronounced than the similarities.

Sources of Hinduism

India is a very large country with many distinct geographic and cultural regions. It has a known history of over five thousand years and even today it is the home of many racially and linguistically different peoples. The forms in which Hinduism appears in various parts of the country are marked by regional and local specificities and exhibit the influence of historical personalities that introduced or reformed religious customs.

As the self-designation *vaidika dharma* would suggest, the 'vedic' element has always been seen as prominent and defining. 'Vedic' refers to the authors of the Veda, who described themselves as *ārya* (noble). In Western scholarly literature the *ārya* became 'Aryans', and the term was used first to define a group of languages that had major affinities and then to establish a racial identity for the peoples using these languages. For over a century it was commonly

Mylapur – street scene at temple entrance

assumed that the fair-skinned 'Vedic Āryans' came to India around 1500 BCE as invaders and settlers, establishing their rule over the dark-skinned natives of India. A great many theories were developed concerning the 'original homeland of the Āryans'. Without any archaeological evidence whatsoever, the Āryans were supposed to have lived originally in the Arctic Circle, in Scandinavia, in today's Ukraine, in Persia, Turkey, or somewhere else in the Middle East or Central Asia. The proof for such migrations was sought and found in linguistic affinities. The languages of the Zoroastrian *Avesta* and the Hindu *Ṛgveda* are indeed strikingly close, and scholars have established common roots for many words in many 'aryan' languages.

The literatures of the Hindus themselves – beginning with the oldest book, the *Ṛgveda* – do not contain any references to a migration of their forefathers from outside India. They do, however, refer to numerous battles against hostile tribes. They celebrate victories over enemies ensconced in forts, and glorify Indra, the most often invoked deity in the *Ṛgveda*, as powerful ally and helper. When in the first decades of our century the ruined cities of Harappa and Mohenjo Daro (in today's Pakistan) were discovered, the missing archaeological evidence for the victorious Āryan invasion of India seemed to have been found. The presumed destruction of these (and other) cities of what became known as the 'Indus civilization' was believed to have taken place around 1750 to 1500 BCE – quite close to the assumed date of the vedic age, arrived at speculatively by assigning a developmental framework to the Veda. The argument lost some of its power when it was found that the Indus civilization had not come to a violent end on account of an invasion from the outside but had slowly ebbed away due to desiccation of the area and major geographic changes.

Meanwhile, further excavations have shown considerable geographical overlap between the area occupied by the Indus civilization (which at its height covered over one million square kilometres!) and the habitats of the Vedic Āryans. There is also cultural continuity. Satellite photography made it possible to identify the dried-out bed of the river Sarasvatī, mentioned as the mightiest of the seven rivers in the area of settlement of the vedic people, which had completely disappeared. It was found that the Sarasvatī, due to tectonic changes in the area, had virtually ceased to carry water by 1900 BCE, 400 years before the Vedic Āryans were supposed to have invaded India. Remnants of many settlements were found along its banks, and it does not make sense to assume that the vedic people built their villages and towns along a dried-out riverbed. Many scholars are inclined to drop the 'invasion theory' and accept the traditional Indian version of an indigenous development. Some Indian scholars also suggest that the Indus valley civilization was a branch of vedic culture. It is too soon to declare vedic India the 'cradle of civilization', as scholars like S. Kak and D. Frawley do, antedating the ancient Mesopotamian and Egyptian civilizations. However, there is no doubt that ancient Indian chronology has to be completely revised and that probably little of the chronology based on the assumed 1500 BCE invasion of India by the Vedic Āryans can be maintained.

In addition to the Veda, which is undoubtedly the major historical source of Hinduism, the traditions of the original inhabitants of India, whose Stone Age culture has been traced back about half a million years, and some of whose practices and beliefs may still be alive among the numerous tribes of *ādivāsīs* (original inhabitants), have influenced Hinduism. Thus it is assumed that the notion of rebirth, so universally accepted today by Hindus, had its origin in animistic tribal notions.

A third component is the very old and highly developed Dravidian culture. It encompassed the entire south of India and is supposed to be older than the Sanskrit-based Northern Vedic culture. There is evidence that Dravidian words, and with them Dravidian cultural notions, were absorbed by the vedic people. Philologists have identified Dravidian elements present in the *Ṛgveda* and in later vedic writings. There is no doubt that many

Dravidian rituals, myths and practices have survived the Aryanization of South India and that South Indian Hinduism has many features not found in the North.

If the Indus civilization, as some claim, is an offshoot of the Vedic culture, one does not have to argue for mutual influences. If it was an independent development, an outpost of Mesopotamian cultures, some findings such as worship of *liṅga* (the phallic symbol associated with Śiva worship) and yoga practices (represented on a seal with a figure interpreted as Śiva Mahāyogi) would indicate an influence on the vedic tradition.

Since Indian culture continued to grow through the millennia, bringing forth such major non-vedic movements as Buddhism and Jainism (to mention only the most prominent ones), Hinduism kept developing and changing as well. Literally hundreds of different religious communities, all with their distinctive beliefs and rituals, developed over the centuries. Their Hindu character was largely restricted to acceptance of the Veda and observance of caste regulations in social contacts. The many invasions to which the Indian subcontinent was subjected also left their traces on Hinduism. Centuries of Muslim domination and 150 years of English colonial rule challenged Hinduism in many ways and produced new movements within it, so that it assimilated some foreign elements but defined itself more narrowly in other respects.

India – the Holy Land of Hinduism

If Hindus speak of *Bhārat Mātā* (Mother India), it is much more than a metaphor or a nationalist slogan: for the Hindu, India is Holy Land. For thousands of years many of its rivers, mountains, cities and groves have been associated, often identified, with deities and events of religious importance. The very names of mountain peaks like Kailāsa or Aruṇācala, of rivers like Ganges and Yamunā, of places like Prāyāga and Kāñcīpuram, of groves like Vṛndāban and Bhādraban suggest to the Hindu the presence of Śiva or Viṣṇu, Devī or Kṛṣṇa. Virtually all older place names have associations with Hindu gods, and so have the proper names of most people. Hinduism is linked in a very literal way to the geography of India.

The *avatāras* (descents, incarnations of God) of Viṣṇu are associated with very specific, real places: the birthplace of Kṛṣṇa in Mathurā and the birthplace of Rāma in Ayodhyā are identified by large temples and have been for many centuries the destination of countless pilgrims. The Muslim invaders knew about the intimate linkage between Hinduism and these sanctuaries, and they not only razed them but built large mosques on top of them. The 're-possession' of the birthplace of Rāma by militant Hindus in December 1992, leading to the destruction of the Bābrī Masjīd (the mosque built over it by Babur) and subsequently to India-wide Hindu-Muslim riots, underscores the importance which localities have for Hinduism.

Hinduism is not just a system of beliefs or a collection of rules but also an intense identification with the many ways in which the sacred is present in India. The country is filled with large and small temples, with wayside shrines and holy places, sometimes marked by a man-made image, sometimes by a stone or a tree. At any given time there are millions of Hindus on pilgrimage to holy sites from which they will take some water or soil to make their own dwellings part of these places. Each of the major holy places has a religious history of its own. Often this is available as a *Sthala Purāṇa*, an account of the miraculous foundation of the place by a god, and a narrative of many miraculous events that have taken place over the centuries. The kinds of stories told and the specific forms of worship practised at each place show great diversity and underscore the importance of locality. Hinduism did not originate from one centre and it is not controlled by a central agency; it consists of a number of complicated networks of local shrines and locally generated beliefs and rituals.

The theme of *Bhārat Mātā*, India as Holy Land of the Hindus, played a great role in the centuries-long struggle for independence. First directed against the Muslims, then against the British, the call to liberate Mother India from the unholy presence of *mlecchas* (foreigners, non-Hindus) was the call for a crusade rather than a simple rebellion. The famous nineteenth-century Bengali writer Bankim Chandra Chatterjee inserted into his historic novel *Ānandamaṭh*, celebrating the famous Samnyāsi Rebellion of 1777 against the Muslims and the British, a paean to Mother India, which became for some time the anthem of the anti-British Indian national movement. In it Chatterjee freely identifies India with the Goddess who had been worshipped in Bengal for ages. The features of India are attributes of the Goddess, and liberating India from foreign domination is the greatest service which a Hindu can do for God. Radical Hindu nationalists even now insist that only those for whom India is Holy Land have a right to live there. They use the term *Hindūtva* ('Hindu-ness') to emphasize a 'non-sectarian' understanding of Hinduism, a Hinduism which all citizens of India are to share.

Is there a religion called Hinduism?

Edward Said's book *Orientalism* has provoked a fierce debate among scholars: Said charges that the picture drawn of the 'Orient' in the West does not reflect Asian reality but Western colonial interests and perspectives. Following him, some scholars have claimed that 'Hinduism' is one of those Orientalist constructs that should be discarded. Realizing that the very name 'Hindu' is of non-Indian origin, that so-called Hindus had a variety of self-designations and that they are divided into multiple communities, worshipping different gods and following diverse customs, one appreciates the merits of the case.

However, the name 'Hindu' as well as the designation 'Hinduism' have by now been taken up by Hindus themselves. In order to distinguish themselves from Muslims, Christians, Parsis, Buddhists, Jains, etc., the worshippers of Viṣṇu, Śiva, Devī and other traditional Indian deities, and the followers of Śaṅkara, Rāmānuja, Ramakrishna, Dayananda and other indigenous Indian teachers call themselves 'Hindu'. While there is de facto a great variety among the various Hindu communities, under the aegis of recent organizations like the Vishwa Hindu Parishad attempts are being made to create a common Hindu ethos, a synthesized mythology and a consciousness of belonging together. *Hindūtva*, 'Hindu-ness', is more than a name: it appeals to many Indians from different sectarian backgrounds, and offers a basis for an indigenization of Indian public life.

In the last fifty years, since India gained independence, much has changed in India along these lines. If Jawaharlal Nehru and his generation of largely foreign-educated leaders had envisioned a development according to a Western pattern – including a belief that economy was the core of a people's aspirations and that economic improvement would take care of communal tensions – the trend today is visibly in a reverse direction. India has no doubt taken over a great deal from Western business and industry. It has become, in many ways, a 'modern' country, with traffic-choked megalopolises, large industrial belts, big airports and huge electricity-generating dams. But it has also remained distinctly Indian at the private and public levels. A whole generation has grown up in free India, proud to be Indian, using Indian languages in schools and offices. The Hindus among them, the vast majority, are also affirming their religious heritage. Participation in Hindu festivals, in Hindu pilgrimages, in Hindu temple rituals has dramatically increased over the last few decades. Attending lectures on the *Bhagavadgītā*, assembling for *satsaṅg*, the chanting of religious hymns in homes, and visiting Hindu holy men and women, have become widespread practices. To call oneself a Hindu definitely means something, and to talk about 'Hinduism' is fully acceptable to Hindus.

As we shall see, defining Hinduism within parameters used, for instance, by Christian churches, is not possible. Rather than reducing Hinduism to notions of 'religion' or 'faith' as they developed in the West, we will have to accept it on its own terms and try to understand its unique character.

Suggested further reading

Allchin, B. and R. Allchin. *The Rise of Civilization in India and Pakistan*. Cambridge University Press: Cambridge, 1982.

Feuerstein, Georg, Subhash Kak and David Frawley. *In Search of the Cradle of Civilization*. Quest Books: Wheaton, Ill., 1995.

Kenoyer, Jonathan Mark. *Ancient Cities of the Indus Valley Civilization*. Oxford University Press: Oxford, 1998.

Majumdar, R. C. (general editor). *The Vedic Age*. Vol. I of *The History and Culture of the Indian People*. 4th ed., Bharatiya Vidya Bhavan: Bombay, 1965.

Nilakantha Sastri, K. A. *The History and Culture of the Tamils*. Firma K. L. Mukhopadhyay: Calcutta, 1964.

Said, Edward. *Orientalism*. Pantheon: London, 1978.

2

The scripture of Hinduism: the Veda

The Veda is the single most important source of Hinduism – acceptance of the Veda as authoritative is the criterion for orthodoxy. Religions like Buddhism and Jainism, which openly reject the Veda and all it implies, are termed *nāstika* (literally 'it is not' people, those for whom the Veda is not ultimate authority), whereas a great variety of schools of thought, however different from each other on many points, are called *āstika* (literally 'it is' people, i.e. accepting the Veda as authoritative) and are deemed orthodox.

To call the Veda 'scripture' is a concession to a Western understanding of religion. The Indian term is *śruti*, meaning 'that which has been perceived through hearing'. For thousands of years, perhaps, the Veda was only transmitted orally, and memorization was the only way to acquire its knowledge. It was supposed to have been originally communicated to the *ṛṣis* (sages) in the form of sound. Writing the text down was considered a desecration. Only after the Muslim invasion was the Veda recorded in writing. Today, of course, it is available in many printed editions and has been translated into many languages, Indian as well as European.

When Hindus speak of the Veda they often mean a much larger body of writings than the Veda in the technical sense. They include also much that has technically been called *smṛti* ('what has been remembered') which is supposed to detail and amplify the often cryptic communications of *śruti*. *Smṛti* literature is immense and varied. Only a small amount of information on it can be provided in the context of this beginner's guide.

From early on Hindus were also aware of the need to interpret rationally the ambiguous statements in their scriptures, to account for apparent contradictions and to devise methods for deriving further guidance from the sources in circumstances not foreseen by them. Thus they developed sophisticated epistemological systems which allowed them to distinguish between different kinds of scriptural statements. They established criteria of truth that were of both theoretical and practical importance in interpreting the Veda and applying it to life-situations.

Śruti – the Veda as revelation

Hindus believe the Veda proper to be without beginning. It was allegedly revealed thousands of years ago to the seers whose names appear in the texts. There are different schools of thought concerning the source of this revelation. The majority of the orthodox would maintain that the Veda is 'impersonal', i.e. not 'Word of God' in the sense in which the Bible is to Jews and Christians, but pre-existent, an embodiment of the eternal law that exists beyond and above any personal law-giver. Some Hindus, however, would perceive the Veda as personal communication from God to chosen seers, the *ṛṣis* of old. They would also extend the notion of *śruti* to include a mass of later writings of a more sectarian nature, often introduced as being the direct communication of Viṣṇu, Śiva or Devī to a specially qualified person.

There is universal agreement that the *Ṛgveda*, a collection of about a thousand fairly short hymns, is the oldest 'text' of Hinduism and the most important Veda. There is, however, a major disagreement on the date of its composition. Considering that the *Ṛgveda* represents a collection of texts ascribed to different family traditions, one would have to assume that some time had to pass before it was completed. Even so, assumptions about its age differ widely. Some Indians claim prehistoric origins – 30,000 BCE – but the majority of Western scholars, following Max Müller (1823–1900), would place it around 1200 BCE. Revisions of dating of the vedic age, as mentioned before, would suggest pushing the date back to at least 2300 BCE, if not earlier.

The term Veda is used in a wider and a narrower sense. In its wider sense, it comprises the four *Saṁhitās* ('collections') namely *Ṛgveda, Yajurveda, Sāmaveda* and *Atharvaveda*; the *Brāhmaṇas* (a large number of very voluminous writings explaining ritual and myths), the *Āraṇyakas* ('forest-treatises'), and the *Upaniṣads*. In its narrower sense, it contains only the four *Saṁhitās*, whose importance has to be understood in connection with the *yajña*, the vedic sacrifice. The Veda is not sacred history or doctrine, not the record of religious experiences or of personal piety, but an essential element of vedic sacrifice, from which, according to the conviction of the ancient Indians, everything depended, including the creation of the world. The *Ṛgveda* provided the *mantras*, the sacred formulas that were indispensable and unchangeable. The *Yajurveda* gave basic instruction concerning the ceremonies to be followed, the *Sāmaveda* suggested the tunes for reciting the hymns, which were effective only if sung at the appropriate pitch. The *Atharvaveda*, which was recognized only later, contains a motley collection of spells and incantations, largely outside the scope of the *yajña*.

If the 'decoding' of the *Ṛgveda* which Subhash Kale has suggested is correct, the text would contain a great deal of astronomical knowledge that was hidden away by the vedic teachers, such as distances of planets from the earth and from each other, their orbits and that of the earth. Direct astronomical references contained in it allow the text to be dated to the third millennium BCE.

The *Ṛgveda* always occupied a special position as *śruti* (revealed authority). Since it is of utmost importance to recite the hymns correctly, a number of auxiliary sciences as well as mnemonic devices were developed. Veda students had to memorize not only the straight text, but also several combinations of syllables, both backwards and forwards. They also had to study the *Vedāngas*

HINDU SCRIPTURES:
ŚRUTI ('Revealed writings') – VEDA (in wider sense)

VEDA – FOUR SAMHITĀS:

Mantra (Saṁhitā):	*Ṛg-Veda*	*Sāma-Veda*	*Yajur-Veda*	*Atharva-Veda*
Brāhmaṇas:	*Aitareya (Aśvalāyana)*	*Tāṇḍya Ṣadviṁśa*	*Taittirīya Śatapatha*	*Gopatha*
Āraṇyakas:	*Aitareya Kauśitakī*		*Bṛhadāraṇyaka Taittirīya*	
Upaniṣads:	*Aitareya Kauśītakī*	*Kena Chāndogya*	*Taittirīya Iśa Kaṭha*	*Praśna Muṇḍaka*

('limbs' or 'extensions' of the Veda) containing rules for pronunciation, ritual, grammar, etymology and astronomy. The latter was important, because the effectiveness of sacrifices depended on precise timing.

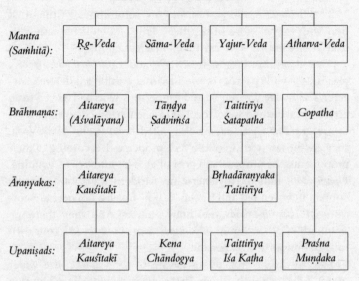

A young brahmin had to undergo many years of training before he was allowed to officiate at a sacrifice. The recitation of the hymns, always at the correct pitch, had to be accompanied by closely prescribed movements of the arms and hands. Because it was believed that a single mistake in pronunciation or a lapse in recitation would nullify the effect of often very costly sacrifices, extreme care was taken to employ only such brahmins as could guarantee a faultless performance. Severe punishments, including expulsion from his caste, awaited a brahmin who either omitted the right movements or failed to follow the right cadences and tunes. Stories are found in Hindu lore that describe how the wrong accenting of a single word at a sacrifice led to disaster for all participants.

The *Brāhmaṇas*, also part of *śruti*, are voluminous writings that deal with explanations of sacrifices. They also contain early versions of myths that were expanded in later centuries.

The *Āraṇyakas* ('forest-treatises'), and the *Upaniṣads* (secret teachings), while part of revealed writing, exhibit a different character. They were written by and for persons who had retired from active social life and were devoted to spiritual practices and mystical insight. The *Upaniṣads* are also called *Vedānta*, end of the Veda: they are the last portion of the Veda proper and, according to their proponents, the purpose and goal of all. The number of 'genuine' *Upaniṣads* is difficult to determine. Modern translations usually contain between ten and fifteen 'major' *Upaniṣads*. There are editions of 108 *Upaniṣads*, the 'holy' number. And then there are hundreds of other, 'minor' *Upaniṣads*, some composed in our own time to honour a great person.

Due to the heterogeneous nature of the Veda (in the wider sense) a distinction has been made since ancient times between *karmakāṇḍa* ('action-part', texts related to sacrifice and ritual) and *jñānakāṇḍa* ('knowledge-part', texts relating to meditation and insight). Proponents of the one tend to minimize the value of the other. The representatives of the *karmakāṇḍa* consider the *jñānakāṇḍa* mere metaphor, not revelation. The adherents of the *jñānakāṇḍa* hold sacrifices to be useless and unable to provide liberation from *saṁsāra*, the cycle of rebirth.

Smṛti – sacred tradition

A large number of books, though not considered 'revealed' in the sense of the Veda, are held to be authoritative on account of their authorship by revered and important figures. Termed *smṛti* (literally 'that which has been remembered', 'tradition'), they are of great practical importance in the lives of Hindus. They contain the rules by which they are to live, and thus have a more immediate impact than *śruti*. The term *smṛti*, too, is used in a narrower and a wider sense. In the narrower sense (which we will adopt here) it comprises the *Dharmaśāstras*, the texts that detail duties and rights of Hindus according to their status. In a wider sense, *smṛti* includes *Itihāsa-Purāṇa*, the great epics *Rāmāyaṇa* and *Mahābhārata*, together with the eighteen *Purāṇas*, Bible-like scriptures which, besides containing myths and legends, also deal with the right behaviour of the followers of various paths. Since *Itihāsa-Purāṇa* is the basis for the various religions that developed in post-vedic times, these works will be dealt with later in more detail.

Among the *smṛtis* in the narrower sense, the *Manu-smṛti* stands out as of particular importance. Manu, according to Hindu tradition, is the forefather of the entirety of present humanity (he survived, through divine intervention, the great flood which killed all humankind), as well as the universal lawgiver. In its first part the book describes the creation of the world and of humankind, i.e. the origin of the four castes. It then deals at great length with rules applying to each caste, duties of individual classes of people, civil and criminal law, sacrifices and atonements, and ends with a description of transmigration and supreme bliss to come. In spite of its great age (dates assigned to it vary from 1200 BCE to 200 BCE) it continues to be of great importance. It has been commented upon by prominent legal authorities throughout the past and its principles are still considered valid in orthodox Hindu circles.

Besides the *Manu-smṛti* there is a large number of others, among which the *Yājñavālkya-smṛti* and the *Viṣṇu-smṛti* are of special importance. Since Hinduism, as said before, is a way of life rather than a 'religion' in the narrow sense, its traditional codes contain the whole range of civil and criminal laws, which in the modern West are deemed to be administered by the state. They also encompass

HINDU SCRIPTURES: SMṚTI ('Tradition')

A. Itihāsa

Rāmāyaṇa

Mahābhārata (Including Bhagavadgītā)

B. Purāṇas

18 Mahāpurāṇas:

6 Vaiṣṇava (sattva) Purāṇas:

Visnu-Purāṇa

Narādīyā-Purāṇa

Bhāgavata-Purāṇa

Garuḍa-Purāṇa

Padma-Purāṇa

Vāraha-Purāṇa

6 Śaiva (rājasa) Purāṇas:

Matsya-Purāṇa

Kūrma-Purāṇa

Liṇga-Purāṇa

Śiva-Purāṇa

Skanda-Purāṇa

Agni-Purāṇa

6 Brahmā (tāmasa) Purāṇas:

Brahmā-Purāṇa

Brahmāṇḍa-Purāṇa

Brahmavaivarta-Purāṇa

Mārkaṇḍeya-Purāṇa

Bhaviṣya-Purāṇa

Vāmana-Purāṇa

18 Upapurānas

Numerous Sthalapurāṇas

C. Dharmaśāstras (= Codes of Law)

Manu-smṛti

Yājñavālkya-smṛti

Viṣṇu-smṛti etc.

religious issues in narrower sense, dealing with such matters as vows and pilgrimages, worship and religious ceremonies. In that sphere they are still indispensable in contemporary India while much of general law is now covered by a secular civil code.

Other authoritative literature

The exigencies of vedic ritual based on *śruti* as well as the vastness of the literature mentioned under *smṛti* required the development of works that condensed and systematized their content. A large number of *sūtras*, 'threads' or compendia, came into existence to summarize in a convenient manner the myriad references to rituals and regulations. They were usually ascribed to an individual author or to a family that wielded a certain authority. Thus the *Śrautasūtras* succinctly describe all aspects of the great public sacrifices to be performed; the *Gṛhyasūtras* deal with rites to be performed in individual homes; the *Dharmasutras* summarize the commandments of traditional vedic religion, and the *Śulvasūtras* give instruction on the building of vedic altars, a kind of applied geometry.

The study of the *Ṛgveda* was compulsory for all young brahmins. However with the passage of centuries, the text became more and more archaic and inaccessible. Thus the need was felt for explanatory literature to cover the various dimensions of Veda study. *Vedāṇgas* (literally 'limbs of the Veda'), auxiliary texts, were developed, each ascribed to an authority. *Śikṣā* deals with correct phonetics (there are vedic sounds and accents that did not exist in later, spoken Sanskrit); *Chandas* explains the often complicated metre of the vedic *sūktas; Vyākaraṇa* offers the rudiments of Sanskrit grammar; *Nirukta* is an etymology of words that had become obsolete and that needed translation into contemporary Sanskrit; *Jyotiṣa* introduced the student to the all-important art of astronomical calculation of the appropriate time for rituals, and *Kalpa* was a primer in ritual know-how.

While Veda in the proper sense was understood to be knowledge that dealt with transcendent matters, 'knowledge' was also required in other fields. Thus a number of *Upavedas*, 'lesser sciences', were developed whose mastery led to what we would call today 'professions'. *Ayur-veda*, 'life-knowledge', medicine, comprised everything that had to do with health, from physical ailments and their cures to advice on how to live in order to ensure a long and prosperous life. *Gandharva-veda*, the science ascribed to the Gandharvas, semi-celestial beings, dealt with dance and music. *Dhanur-veda* taught the art of archery, while *Sthāpatya-veda* was the basis for architecture and sculpture.

With the development of what has been called 'sectarian Hinduism', i.e. the growth of communities (*sampradāyas*) focusing their devotion on one particular deity, a need was felt to provide scriptural legitimation to the specific teachings and forms of worship of each. Thus many works originated which, purporting to be direct revelation from the mouth of either Viṣṇu, Śiva or Devī, provided the foundation for the doctrines and rituals of specific sects. *Saṁhitās* ('collections', not to be confused with the vedic *Samhitās*, the collection of vedic hymns) are treated like *śruti* by Vaiṣṇavas, *Āgamas* ('scriptures') by Śaivas, and *Tantras* ('looms' or 'threads') by Śāktas. These works are usually very voluminous and very large in number. There are literally hundreds of them, most of which have not even appeared in print, and even fewer of which are available in English.

Pramāṇa – interpretation of sacred texts

Besides revelation and tradition, Hindus have always used rational examination as means to arrive at religiously relevant truth. Logical examination was needed to clarify obscure passages in revelation, to harmonize contradictions in tradition and to extend the application

HINDU SCRIPTURES: OTHER AUTHORITATIVE LITERATURE

A. Sūtras:
   1. Śṛautasūtras
   2. Grhyasūtras
   3. Dharmasūtras
   4. Śulvasūtras

B. Vedāṅgas (Auxiliary sciences connected with Veda-study):
   1. Śikṣā (Phonetics)
   2. Chandas (Metre)
   3. Vyākaraṇa (Grammar)
   4. Nirukta (Etymology)
   5. Jyotiṣa (Astronomy)
   6. Kalpa (Ritual)

C. Upavedas (sciences not connected with Veda-study):
   1. Ayur-veda (Medicine)
   2. Gandharva-veda (Music and dancing)
   3. Dhanur-veda (Archery)
   4. Sthāpatya-veda (Architecture)

D. Sectarian scriptures
   1. Saṁhitās (Vaiṣṇava)
   2. Āgamas (Śaiva)
   3. Tantras (Śākta)

of revelation and tradition to new areas. Since ultimately all religious knowledge derives from the revealed word of the Veda one could say that all later developments of Hindu religion and philosophy are but an interpretation of this *śabda* (word). Indian thinkers have devoted a great amount of energy and acumen to interpretation, and the greatest works of India's creative philosophers are commentaries on scriptures. Over the course of the centuries three such scriptures were selected as most authoritative: the (principal) *Upaniṣads*, the *Bhagavadgītā* and the *Brahmasūtras*. This triad of proof-texts (*prasthāna trāyī*) had to be commented upon by anyone claiming the title of *ācārya* ('master'). The commentaries, needless to say, are often many times longer than the texts themselves and constitute the real substance of the various philosophical schools.

Vedic interpretation in the more precise sense, i.e. the exegesis of the hymns of the *Ṛgveda*, is one of the most difficult and most controversial fields of study. Since the time of its composition is so remote and its language so archaic, there are many questions which probably will never find a satisfactory answer. Even in Indian antiquity a need was felt to provide a glossary of obsolete words: the *Nirukta* by *Yāska* (*c.* 500 BCE) did this with the admission that the Veda was no longer understood as 'normal' speech but only as a fixed sequence of sounds whose meaning was beyond recovery. Consequently, very few Indian authors attempted an interpretation of the meaning of the verses of the *Ṛgveda*, and restricted themselves to dealing with formalisms. Traditional Indian hermeneutic rules suggest three alternatives from which an interpreter can freely choose: one can understand the hymns as relating to sacrificial rites, to deities, or to the Self. While the text of the Veda had to be respected as ultimate authority, its interpretation was left completely open. In our own time an interesting suggestion was made by Subhash Kak, a computer engineer with a vast background in Indian studies. He claims that the *Ṛgveda* contains, in an encoded manner, the vast astronomical knowledge of the vedic Indians. He calls it a 'Stonehenge in words' and claims to have rediscovered the code which was lost about 3000 years ago.

The *Manu-smṛti* threatens horrible punishment to brahmins who divulge the Veda to persons not authorized to listen to it, not to mention learning it. For many centuries – perhaps even millennia – this secrecy was maintained, and for several centuries Europeans who had heard about the Veda and wished to know more about it were refused instruction. It was only in the nineteenth century, under British administration, that Indian pandits began to share their knowledge of Sanskrit and Veda with Europeans. European Indology, apart from the practical uses which it had for the British administration in India, was motivated largely by a historical urge: there was a search for origins, and for some time Sanskrit was held to be the original language of humankind from which all other languages were derived. European scholars were also intrigued by the immense age which Indians attributed to their Veda. It was one of the triumphs of Western humanistic scholarship when Max Muller succeeded, over a period of more than a quarter of a century, in collating and printing the text of the *Ṛgveda* together with the mediaeval Sanskrit commentary by Sāyaṇa. As far as the content of the *Ṛgveda* was concerned, Max Müller felt rather disappointed. He thought many of the hymns crude and childish and read into others a vague kind of nature-mysticism. Lacking the traditional background, European scholars tried to appreciate the 'lyrics' without understanding the vital reference of the *sūktas* (hymns) to the Vedic sacrifice.

While the meaning of some of the hymns appears to be quite intelligible – hymns dealing with the creation of the world, or with the power of the word; hymns eulogizing the beauty of dawn, or the power of Indra – others are virtually inaccessible, not only to outsiders, but also to Indians who are familiar with their own tradition. As a matter of fact, the pandits who recite vedic hymns

TO EARTH

Earth, you bear the heavy mountains.
You quicken, with your many streams, the soil.
Our songs of praise are celebrating you,
Expansive, bringing forth the clouds.

You are bright, and you hold fast
The forest trees in the ground,
When rain pours down from the skies,
Lightning rending your clouds.

Ṛgveda V, 84

that are still used for rites of passage often do not know their meaning, and the meaning, when known, often has little obvious relation to the rituals. The basis of Hinduism may be vedic, but the people's actual beliefs and the doctrines of religious teachers are rarely derived from the Vedas. They usually are found in *Itihāsa-Purāṇa* and in the *Darśanas* that developed in post-vedic times.

The power of the revealed word

In our present culture words are meant to convey meaning, and they are found meaningful only to the extent that they carry intelligible, useful information. That was apparently not always so, and in the Veda we encounter a text where words were intended to embody power regardless of intellectual meaning. *Brahman*, the supreme power, was held to be identical with the word of the Veda, and the prestige which brahmins enjoyed was derived from their being the custodians and mediators of the Veda. The word of the vedic hymns was the secret which made sacrifices successful and fulfilled the wishes of the sacrificer.

Many *mantras* that are used to create power and to influence deities have no discernible word-meaning. They are meaningless syllables whose power derives from their being revealed. The best known and most potent of these mantras is OM (AUM), also called *prāṇava*. OM is not a concept, not a designation of something; it is the 'all-word', as the *Chāndogya Upaniṣad* says. Representing the sum total of all letters of the alphabet, it embodies all things in the form of sound, it is *śabdabrahman*, the supreme in the form of the word. All recitations of religious scriptures are initiated and concluded with the sounding of OM. It is printed at the beginning and end of all religious books, it is engraved over entrances to temples and ashrams and adorns many a private home as well.

The notion that all sacred texts are mantras, that besides a possibly understandable meaning and teaching they have a mysterious non-verbal power, is very widespread in India. Many sacred books themselves encourage such an understanding when they promise merit for uttering even fragments of their contents and suggest that the mere preservation of a verse or chapter of the sacred book draws down blessings to a home where they are kept. This belief is also the basis for a widespread contemporary practice found all over India today: the public recitation, usually over loudspeakers, of entire religious books like the *Rāmcaritmanas* or the *Bhāgavatam*. Even if nobody listens or nobody understands a word because of other loudspeakers blaring forth other recitations, the sponsor of such a recitation is believed not only to gain merit for himself but also to generate blessings for the community into which the texts are broadcast: the power of the sacred word acts independently and unfailingly.

Suggested further reading

Coward, Harold and Krishna Sivaraman (eds). *Revelation in Indian Thought*. Dharma Publishing: Emeryville, Calif., 1977.

Gonda, Jan. *Vedic Literature*. Vol. 1, fasc. 1 of *History of Indian Literature*. Harrassowitz: Wiesbaden, 1975.

— *The Ritual Sutras*. Vol. 1, fasc. 2 of *History of Indian Literature*. Harassowitz: Wiesbaden, 1977.

Renou, Louis. *Vedic India*. Susil Gupta: Calcutta, 1957.

3

The vedic ordering of life

Hinduism, like other 'totalizing' religions, aimed not only to shape society but also to control all aspects of an individual's life. In addition to structuring society according to caste, it structured the lifetime of its adherents and their daily routine. The name for this ordering of life, *varṇāśramadharma*, contains references to this: vedic *dharma* consists in

- observing rights and duties according to one's *varṇa* (social stratum)
- following in one's personal life the prescribed sequence of *āśramas* (stages in life).

This is the subject of what follows.

A day in the life of a Hindu

Before going into detail it should be noted that most of the rules that govern the life of a Hindu apply to males of the higher castes only. Vedic religion, as it appears in the texts we possess, became increasingly patriarchal, and later Hinduism clearly disadvantaged women in many respects. It hardly makes any sense to use inclusive language when dealing with the Vedic life order, because most, if not all of it, concerns men only. (Devised many centuries ago for a mostly rural India, the 'ideal routine of life' can only be upheld in a modified manner by most contemporary Hindus.)

In Hinduism much of what is nowadays called hygiene is part of the religious routine, and consequently surrounded by many regulations. A Hindu householder is to rise at dawn (before sunrise) and to utter, before speaking to anyone, the name of his *Iṣṭa-devatā*, the deity of his choice. He should then look at the palms of his hands to make sure that the first thing he beholds is an 'auspicious' object. Similarly, he should then touch the earth so as to perform an 'auspicious' action before doing anything else. After bowing to the images of deities in his room and muttering mantras, he is to think about the day's agenda with a view to increasing *dharma* (righteousness) and *artha* (wealth).

Daily hygiene is surrounded by a great many regulations that have to be kept religiously. In our day and age we appreciate the 'ecological' wisdom contained in many of these rules, which ensured that pollution of water was prevented. The daily bath, a physical necessity in a hot country, is also a prescribed daily ritual for Hindus. The books detail how it is to be performed and what mantras have to be muttered while pouring the water. A special ritual, called *tarpaṇa*, still widely practised, deserves mention: while taking one's bath in a river, one is to fold both hands and scoop up some water. While releasing it back into the river one is to recite mantras to please the deities and the deceased ancestors. After that, most Hindus would apply to their forehead and other parts of the body markings of coloured clay or sandalpaste, expressing their affiliation to a particular *saṁprādaya* (religious community). Those markings are taken quite seriously – without them all ceremonies and prayers are believed to be fruitless.

The morning prayer, called *saṁdhyā* ('twilight'), which follows, is still observed by many millions of Hindus every day. The main text is the age-old *gāyatrī-mantra*, which is repeated several times. Many will add hymns to their chosen deity and readings from sacred books, and do *pūjā* (worship) by waving lights and camphor, burning incense sticks and prostrating themselves before the images of deities. Most Hindu homes would have either a room exclusively used for worship, or at least a corner in the living-room where images are kept and worshipped. The rituals to be used in *pūjā*, often quite elaborate, are different for each *saṁpradāya* and have to be executed correctly and in precise order to have the desired effect.

The daily morning worship – to be followed up by rituals at noon and in the evening – is the redemption of the first of the five 'debts' that Hindus believe humans are born with: debts towards the deities, the sages, one's teachers and parents, humankind in general, and all living beings. The deities have to be satisfied with worship, the sages by study of scriptures, teachers and parents by gifts, humankind in general by feeding guests, and all living beings by giving the left-overs from meals to animals.

Brahmins were supposed to spend most of their time in worship and study; non-brahmins were encouraged to give gifts to brahmins to maintain them. Hospitality is a time-honoured custom among Hindus and turning away a guest, especially if he is a holy man, is considered a grave sin. There are many popular stories that tell of the evil consequences of such an action. The most popular story in this connection is the one about Daridra-Nārāyaṇa: God himself, in the guise of a beggar, asks for a meal in a village. He is turned away by all the well-to-do people, but welcomed to the hut of the poorest, who would rather starve himself than let a guest go hungry. As one would expect, the beggar reveals himself to be Viṣṇu Nārāyaṇa, the Lord, who amply rewards his host with riches and blessings.

The fulfilment of one's duty towards all creatures can range from feeding a left-over *cāpāti* (Indian flat bread) to a cow on the street, to building elaborate *gośālas*, homes for old cattle, who are fed and cared for till they die a natural death. Such nursing homes, often established by rich merchants, can be found in many places in India today – certainly a very touching and noble undertaking, making up for the many acts of cruelty committed against animals by humankind.

The four stages of life

In addition to regulating the daily routine and prescribing in detail each and every action to be done or avoided, the Hindu way of life also contains a structure that divides a Hindu's entire life into four stages (*āśramas*). These stages are related to the four aims of life (*puruṣārthas*), which constitute a full and meaningful life. These four aims are:

- the practice of righteousness (*dharma*)
- the acquisition of material wealth (*artha*)
- the enjoyment of sensual pleasure (*kāma*)
- the attainment of final liberation (*mokṣa*).

Accordingly, life is divided into four successive stages, devoted to the realization of these values.

1. Student

The first stage is studenthood (*brahmacarya*). Childhood as such is supposed to be a time of complete freedom and without any obligations whatsoever. With initiation (*upanayana*), usually between the ages of eight and twelve, both education and moral responsibility begin. While nowadays most Hindu children (at least in the cities) follow a curriculum of education that is hardly different from that in any Western country, formerly brahmin boys moved after initiation into the family of a *guru* (preceptor) for twelve years of training and service. Even now, after *upanayana* (the initiation ceremony) many Hindu families have their young boys taught on a regular basis by a religious teacher – often the grandfather – who introduces the child into the family traditions. During the years of studenthood the young brahmin leads an ascetic life and spends most of his time in study.

2. Householder

Normally the time of studenthood ends with marriage, and the young man then enters the stage of the householder (*gṛhastya*), when he is supposed to devote his time to the acquisition and increase of wealth. He should enjoy his life, procreate children, but also observe *dharma* (the law of rightousness), the pillar of social life. A householder has obligations not only towards his family but also towards society at large, and he must support its major institutions. When his children have become adults he is supposed to hand over all his wordly business and to withdraw from society.

3. Forest-Dweller

He then enters the stage of 'forest-dweller' (*vānaprasthya*). Together with his wife, if she is still alive, he is to move out of the village to the fringe of the nearby forest and devote himself to the pursuit of non-wordly activities.

4. Renouncer

The last years of life are to be spent in renunciation of everything (*saṁnyāsa*) – homeless and possessionless, wandering as a mendicant from one holy place to the next until death comes. This is the pursuit of *moksa* (liberation), the highest and ultimate aim of life.

While very few married people today follow the pattern of *vānaprasthya* and *saṁnyāsa*, there are large numbers of *saṁnyāsis* and *saṁnyāsinīs* in today's India, men and women who have chosen a life of celibacy and mendicancy in pursuit of liberation and salvation. There are many millions of such *sādhus* (literally 'good, holy persons', roughly comparable to 'monks' and 'nuns') who are organized in hundreds of different orders, each with their own elaborate rules and regulations. While the original meaning of

THE STUDENT

A young man who has been duly initiated, must offer daily fuel to the sacred fire, beg food, sleep on the ground and help his teacher.

Every day, having bathed and being purified, he must offer libations of water to the gods, sages and ancestors, worship the images of the gods, and place fuel on the sacred fire.

He must abstain from honey, meat, perfumes, garlands, spices, women, acids, and from injuring living beings.

He must not anoint his body, put collyrium on his eyes, use shoes or umbrella.

He must abstain from desire, anger, covetousness, dancing, singing, and making music.

He must not indulge in gambling, idle disputes, backbiting, lying, looking at and touching women, hurting others.

The teacher is the image of Brahman, the father is the image of Prajāpati, the mother is the image of the earth, an elder brother is the image of oneself.

By honouring his mother he gains this world, by honouring his father the middle sphere, by honouring his teacher the world of Brahman.

The teacher is ten times more venerable than his assistant, the father a hundred times more than the teacher, but the mother a thousand times more than the father.

The vow of studying the three Vedas under a teacher must be maintained for thirty-six years, or for half that time, or for a quarter, or until the student has perfectly memorized them.

Manu-smṛti, VII

saṁnyāsa implied a life of constantly moving from place to place (only during the four months of the rainy season, the *cāturmāsa*, was the *saṁnyāsi* allowed to stay put), and no possessions except for some pieces of clothing, a water vessel, and a cup to receive food, most *sādhus* today are affiliated to a monastery in which they spend most of their time, with their own rooms, some modest possessions like books and basic furniture, and regular meals supplied by the institution or its benefactors.

A rather recent phenomenon are the *saṁnyāsis* who go abroad to collect funds and disciples, and who often surround themselves with luxury: big comfortable ashrams, fast cars, electronic gadgets and so on. They themselves, as well as their faithful followers, do not find anything incongruous in this. They claim to represent God and feel entitled to accept honour and gifts on God's behalf.

The four *varṇas*: castes and sub-castes

The oldest Hindu creation myth, the *Puruṣasūkta* of the *Ṛgveda*, describes the origin of humankind as the result of the sacrifice of a cosmic human-shaped being, the *puruṣa*. From its head came the *brahmins*, from its arms the *kṣatriyas*, from its thighs the *vaiśyas*, and from its legs the *śūdras*. This myth is foundational for Hindu society and is repeated time and again in different versions throughout Hindu literature. It is designed to prove that the original caste division is natural, based on creation, and God-willed. Texts like the *Manu-smṛti* treat the myth as a fact, and proceed to derive from it not only the notion of a hierarchical subordination of castes but also the basic rights and duties of all those who belong to each one of the divisions. Thus:

- *Brahmins* were to be the custodians of the sacred word of the Veda and the rituals required for the good of society. They were to be honoured by all and supported materially through gifts and grants. In Western society they would correspond to the professional clergy.
- *Kṣatriyas*, excelling through physical strength and courage, were to be warriors and rulers. They had to defend their country and

to protect its citizens. In return they had the right to receive part of the goods and services produced by the rest of society. They roughly correspond to the nobility of pre-modern Europe.

- *Vaiśyas* were to be the backbone of the economy: business people, agriculturalists, craftsmen, people devoted to creating and augmenting wealth. In modern terms they would be the middle class.
- *Śūdras*, the large mass of virtually unpropertied labourers, servants and menials, formed the base of Hindu society. Their task was to serve the three higher castes, who were collectively called *dvījas* ('twiceborn') because they were supposed to have undergone a second birth through the ceremony of initiation, where they received the sacred thread as a sign of distinction.

The *caturvarṇa* ('four classes') system also expressed a religious hierarchy: people were born into their respective castes on account of the *karma* that they had accumulated in previous lives. Brahmins were born into the highest caste because of great merit – *Śūdras* were born into the lowest caste in order to atone for alleged misdeeds.

While the *caturvarṇa* class-division scheme provides the overall structure of Hindu society, the actual division into more than 3000 *jātīs* ('birth-groups', usually translated as 'sub-castes') makes caste a much more complex affair. There are hundreds of *jātīs* within each *varṇa* and the local ranking is not always the same. With each *jātī* having its own restrictions on intermarrying and sharing food, social relationships in Hindu society are anything but simple. It is not true, as many outsiders seem to believe, that the Indian Constitution abolished caste. It abolished 'untouchability', made it a punishable offence to disadvantage people for belonging to a so-called 'scheduled caste', for being outcastes. Caste regulations provided exclusion as punishment for certain violations of caste rules. With the passage of time about a quarter of all Hindus came to belong to the 'outcasts', who had quite literally no rights whatsoever: they had to dwell outside the villages and towns, were not allowed to use public wells or tanks, were restricted to doing the most degrading work. While many reformers in the nineteenth century attacked the institution of caste as such and wanted to see it abolished, Mahatma Gandhi concentrated his crusade on the abolition of untouchability. Instead of calling the outcastes *nihspṛśya* (untouchable) he termed them *Hari-jan* ('God's people'). Independent India accepted Gandhi's demand to do away with untouchability, and made it part of its Constitution. Yet in daily life Harijans still have to suffer many indignities and cruelties. Caste is alive and well in today's India. Most deputies to parliaments at all levels are elected on the basis of caste-majorities in their constituencies and most marriages are still arranged along caste compatibilities.

Although one's *jātī* (caste) is determined by birth, a certain amount of upward and downward mobility is possible. Marrying a partner from another caste always implied that the children belonged to the lower caste of the two. Similarly, certain infringements of caste regulations were sanctioned by either lowering of caste status or by complete excommunication. On the other hand, one could buy or otherwise gain higher caste standing. Many *rājas*, petty Hindu kings, originally came from low castes and had their genealogies reconstructed in order to prove themselves *kṣatriyas*.

In our own time many people from low castes, or even outcastes, have risen to prominent positions in professions and politics. Lately India even elected a former outcaste, K. R. Narayan, to its highest public office, that of President. Harijans who made it were usually helped by organizations that worked for the advancement of outcastes and low-castes. In the 1980s the Indian government enacted legislation which guarantees a certain number of places in schools and positions in administration to people coming from these strata of society.

The former outcastes, formerly called untouchables, later renamed members of 'scheduled castes', and called Harijans by

Gandhi, have recently chosen to call themselves *Dalits* (oppressed) and have organized themselves so as to exercise political and economic influence. They are fast becoming a major force on the Indian scene, and are quite articulate in expressing their aims and demands. Among them are highly educated and experienced organizers with visions of freedom and equality of opportunity. Often organized along lines of religious affiliation, they receive support from religious bodies, although they try to keep independent, and distance themselves from Hinduism.

While some of the regulations of the *catur-varṇa-āśrama-dharma* are obviously no longer tenable, there are many in India today who defend the underlying principles. They hold that a division of society into classes is natural and that the Indian schema, basing class distinctions on merit and function, is superior to one based on money and economic clout, as in the West. They also see value in structuring life with a spiritual goal in mind: without denying the legitimacy of enjoying material values, the Hindu conception gives priority to spiritual emancipation and reaching a transcendent goal.

Suggested further reading

Derret, J. D. M. *History of Indian Law* (Dharmasāśtra). Brill: Leiden, 1973.

Dumont, Emile. *Homo Hierarchicus*. University of Chicago Press: Chicago, 1970.

Kosambi, D. D. *An Introduction to the Study of Indian History*. Popular Book Depot: Bombay, 1956.

Pandey, R. B. *Hindu Samskaras: Socio-Religious Study of the Hindu Sacraments*. Motilal Banarsidass: Delhi, 1969.

4

Vedic ritual

The most outstanding feature of vedic religion is its ritual: domestic and public sacrifices and life-cycle rituals encompassed everything, ensuring conformity with the all-ordering law of the universe expressed in *dharma*. While much of vedic religion has been replaced by Puranic beliefs and practices, an astonishingly large amount of vedic ritual has survived and has become an integral part of Hinduism. This chapter deals first with the largely historical practice and theory of *yajña* (sacrifice), and then provides information about the universally practised *samskāras* (sacraments) that still furnish the framework for the life of a modern Hindu.

The vedic sacrifice

According to one school of thought, the entire Veda served the sole purpose of providing formulae and ritual guidance for the performance of the *yajña* (sacrifice) which was considered indispensable for the existence and the well-being of the vedic people. So crucial was sacrificial practice in the mind of the vedic Indians that they believed the creation of the world itself to have been caused by a primordial sacrifice of a primaeval being. Similarly, the orderly progress of the universe had to be kept in motion by sacrifices performed at crucial junctures: new moon and full moon, solstice and the beginning of a new solar year, eclipses and other unusual events. It was formerly the duty of kings to arrange for public sacrifices for the well-being of their people. While for many centuries public vedic sacrifices had almost completely ceased to be performed, they are apparently on the increase again. Usually under the patronage of rich merchants, groups of brahmins are frequently employed to build fire-altars according to vedic patterns and to perform sacrifices in keeping with age-old rituals.

The construction of altars with bricks of particular shapes, the preparation and the performance of the sacrifice itself were very complex, leading to the development of a veritable science that had to be mastered by the adepts before they were allowed to practise. Modern research has found interesting numerical proportions in the numbers of bricks required for each layer, the number of layers and the number of officiants, indicating probably a fairly detailed and advanced astronomical knowledge. Vedic ritual texts themselves frequently equate the sacrifice with the year, a month and a day, and the time at which particular sacrifices have to be offered is set according to strict astronomical parameters.

The efficacy of the sacrifice further depended on the kind of offering made. The noblest sacrifice, according to vedic texts, was a human victim. Next came a horse, the so-called *aśvamedha* which is celebrated in many famous texts. It was the crowning ritual of a pretender to a throne and involved a number of rites extending over a year, culminating in the ritual slaughter of a horse. It was celebrated for many centuries; the last one seems to have been performed by an eighteenth-century Rājput king. The animal most frequently sacrificed was the goat. Some animals, like camels, were excluded: they did not possess *medha*, the substance that made the sacrifice work. Also non-animal matter such as animal- or human-shaped figures made of dough, or liquids such as the famous *soma* (the fermented, intoxicating juice of an unknown plant) were offered.

A large class of texts called *Śrautasūtras* deals with the performance of public sacrifices at which often hundreds of animals were slaughtered and thousands of brahmins invited to receive gifts. Since the efficacy of the sacrifice depended on the correct pronunciation of the mantra and the exact execution of each prescribed ceremony the performance of sacrifice became the domain of specialists who had to undergo many years of training.

Another kind of text, the so-called *Gṛhyasūtras*, regulated the domestic rituals that had to be performed by brahmin householders. At these rituals it was usually rice, barley cakes, milk and curds that were offered to the divine powers, the *devas*.

The Hindu sacraments

There are a number of rituals called *saṁskāras* (usually translated as 'sacraments'), performed for the benefit of individuals, which are required to make a Hindu (of the three higher castes) a full member of his community. They begin at conception and end with the rites following cremation, and are meant to 'sanctify the body and purify it in this life and after death', as the *Manu-smṛti* has it. Whereas in former times there was a large number of such *saṁskāras*, nowadays only a few are practised. But they are considered of supreme importance in the life of every higher-caste Hindu.

Birth

In former times the very conception of a child was surrounded by ceremonies, and during pregnancy a number of rites were performed. Today the first *saṁskāra* is performed at birth. It includes the giving of a name and the establishment of a horoscope, which is of crucial importance in the determination of the auspicious time for many undertakings throughout the child's life.

Initiation

The next *saṁskāra* is *upanayana* (initiation), considered the 'second birth', accompanied by the investiture with the sacred thread (*janëu*). It marks the end of childhood and the introduction of the initiate into Hindu society. It seemed to have been given to both boys and girls in the earliest times and was then restricted to males only for many centuries. Lately some women activists have begun to give the *janëu* to young females too. Formally the newly initiated young Hindu would begin the first of the four stages of life, *brahmacarya* (studenthood), and stay with a teacher for twelve years. Nowadays *upanayana* usually means that the young boy receives instruction in his tradition from a pandit. The ceremony itself is quite elaborate and retains many features of an ancient rite of passage that involved quite serious risks. Even liberal Hindu families usually have their boys undergo *upanayana* and continue wearing the sacred thread that marks them off as belonging to the *dvījātis* (the 'twice-born').

Marriage

The most important *saṁskāra* for all Hindus is marriage, which for women used to be the only sacrament. It is the religious and social high point in a Hindu's life and is celebrated with lavish feasts. The religious ceremony varies from one part of India to another but contains many ancient Vedic mantras and rituals. The marriage ceremonies are to ensure fidelity, happiness and progeny. If something goes wrong in a marriage people will often search for flaws in the marriage ritual and blame it on those. The marriage ritual underscores the importance of the woman of the house – she is called 'half of man' – and the domestic rituals cannot be performed without her. Traditionally it was the great desire of every Hindu to have a son. Apart from continuing the family, the (eldest) son had many religious functions as well. Even the etymology of the word *putra* (son) was explained as being derived from 'hell (*put*), 'saviour (*tra*)'. The last rites could only be performed by a male descendant: without these the deceased would forever remain *pretas*, restless ghosts. There is, however, a rite to 'deem' a daughter a 'son' for the last rites, when no male offspring is available. Today it is not uncommon for daughters to perform the last rites if the deceased had no son.

Death

Similar in importance and universally observed are the last rites accompanying death and concerning afterlife. Most Hindus cremate their dead. Exceptions are only small children, *saṁnyāsis* (ascetics) and the followers of some sects like the *Vīraśaiva*, who practise burial. The body is washed, hair and nails are clipped, a shroud is placed around the body and flowers are heaped on it. It is usually carried to the cremation grounds within hours; a procession of relatives and friends accompanies the bier, chanting *Rām nām satya hai*, 'the name of Rāma is truth'. The eldest son of the deceased has to light the pyre. While it is burning, lengthy portions of the Vedic hymns for the dead are recited. Yama, the lord of the netherworlds, is invoked to prepare for the deceased a good place among his ancestors. Agni, the god of fire, is requested to carry the departed safely into the realm of the fathers. The earth is beseeched to be good to the dead. Old taboos are still observed in connection with cremation rites. Dealing with corpses causes ritual impurity, and so all those associated with the funeral have to undergo purification ceremonies before rejoining society. For a full year ceremonies have to be continued at certain intervals in order to ensure the safe and final passage from this life into the next.

While the death ritual of Hindus today retains many features of ancient vedic traditions, the actual beliefs of Hindus are strongly shaped by puranic influences. Vedic ritual contains no hint of karma and rebirth, beliefs which so strongly colour the worldview of later Hinduism. According to ancient vedic tradition the departed male of an upper caste would join his forefathers – after proper performance of *śrāddha* (the last rites) – and enjoy afterlife on the cool moon. There is place on the ancestor lists for only three generations: once the great-grandson of an ancestor dies, the ancestor is eliminated from the list and ceases to receive oblations. The newer and virtually universally accepted notions of death and afterlife assume that according to his or her karma, a Hindu will be reborn sooner or later in another body. If all karma has been eliminated, liberation from rebirth has been accomplished, the highest aim of all.

The meaning of Karma

Vedic ritual religion constitutes the core of what is called *karmamārga*, the 'Path of Work'. Karma in its original meaning is synonymous with (vedic) sacrifice and its effects, which were believed to be infallible. An entire philosophical school of thought, *Mīmāmsā*, occupied itself with proving this point. To begin with, it assumed that the Veda itself, on whose authority the whole tradition rests, is not based on any personal utterances, human or divine, but has an eternal existence of its own. Thus no mediation that could possibly distort or falsify it intervenes between its source and its effects. The *Brāhmaṇas* repeatedly say that one who desires heaven should perform the *agniṣṭoma*, a particular type of vedic sacrifice. Many people apparently did so. Why, then, someone might ask, do the persons who performed this sacrifice still find themselves on earth? Is there something wrong with that promise? No, say the *Mīmāṁsakas*, the most orthodox interpreters of the Veda: the sacrifice produces some kind of invisible substance, the *apūrva*, which precedes the sacrificer to heaven and becomes available to him when he dies. Then, like a heavenly bank-account, it will benefit him for as long as it lasts. When it is used up he has to return to earth.

With the Upanisads and their criticism of vedic sacrifice as a leaky boat, unable to carry a person across the ocean of *saṁsāra* (the ever-repeating cycle of world-events), a new meaning of *karma* arises: etymologically derived from the root *kṛ* (to make, to do), karma now is extended to mean all human activities and their consequences. An action not only has an effect on the outside world, it also leaves an imprint on the actor. Good deeds leave a positive imprint, bad deeds a negative one. Joined to the notion of rebirth – an almost necessary corollary to the understanding of the world as an ever self-repeating process (*saṁsāra*) – the accumulated karma of a lifetime determines the next bodily existence. Good karma results in a birth into a higher caste, a healthy body, a wealthy family, perhaps even as a superhuman being, a *deva*, a sojourn in heaven. Bad karma could lead to rebirths not only in less desirable human circumstances, but also as animals or in hells.

Texts like the *Manu-smṛti* provide long lists that describe what kind of rebirth would be the punishment for a particular sin. They also explain that bodily defects and deformities like lameness, black teeth, or ill health, are the consequences of bad karma accumulated in earlier lives. Bad karma can even lead to punishment in hells. While Hindus know a great number of hells with specific punishments for great sinners, none of them is eternal. If people who have committed a sin are wise, they will, during their lifetime, atone for their sin and thus save themselves the consequences of karma. The authoritative religious texts, the *śāstras*, have lengthy catalogues matching sins with appropriate *prāyaścittas* (atonements). The most frequent forms of penance are fasting, muttering certain formulae, bathing and otherwise mortifying oneself. For the most severe crimes the only atonement is self-inflicted death.

When the religious communities of Vaiṣṇavas, Śaivas, Śāktas and others arose, they again modified the understanding of karma and rebirth. They usually introduced a new ethos in which sectarian practices were given prominence: the observance of certain feasts in honour of the deity, the application of certain external marks as a sign of submission to a particular god, affiliation with believers of the same kind, became important and were the presupposition for acquiring good karma. Not only this, God's grace was able to annul the bad karma of a person who had shown signs of contrition. Often the mere invocation of the name of the god, or the symbolic sacrifice of a leaf or some fruit, would be sufficient to wipe away the consequences of karma and transport the person into heaven.

Another, and perhaps more far-reaching, transformation of the notion of karma is found in the famous *Bhagavadgītā*, accepted by many Hindus as God's own revelation to humankind. Taking up earlier notions of karma, Kṛṣṇa teaches in the *Gītā* the way of *niṣkāma karma* ('desireless action'). The context of this teaching is a serious ethical dilemma faced by Arjuna, the protagonist of the *Gītā*. As the leader of the Pāndavas he finds himself in a situation where war seems to be the only way to determine succession to a throne which had been usurped by a rival faction of the family, the Kauravas. While personally inclined to forgo his right to succession and to leave the kingdom to his cousins, Arjuna is admonished by Kṛṣṇa that such a solution would not only bring discredit to him and make him appear a coward, but would also result in his and his family's karmic downfall. When Arjuna, citing traditional law, expresses his fear that killing relations and elders will lead to punishment in hell, Kṛṣṇa offers a new solution to this ethical dilemma. Actions, he says, result in bad karma only if done out of bad motives like greed or hatred. If an action is performed only for the sake of fulfilling righteousness, if a deed is done in order solely to do one's duty, this action does not result in karma. Desireless action, performing one's duty regardless of loss or gain, not only saved Arjuna from his predicament, but is seen by many Hindus today as the highest ethical ideal.

At the beginning of the twentieth century B. G. Tilak, one of the most articulate advocates of Indian independence from British rule, used the *Bhagavadgītā* as 'The Gospel of Action' to propagate the idea of actively fighting for freedom as a religious duty of Hindus. Mahatma Gandhi took this notion up and gave a new meaning to the ancient *karmamārga*, equating it with engagement for the good of the country and one's fellow humans.

Revival of vedic ritual

Western scholars, from the beginning of their investigation into Ancient India, had focused on the study of vedic ritual. Vedic ritual texts were the oldest, and from a historical standpoint, the most interesting. They also offered a self-contained, sophisticated system of interlocking elements, and were removed from the vicissitudes of change and re-interpretation. Vedic rituals, except in the context of the *saṁskāras* (sacraments), had ceased to be performed and were no longer part of living Hinduism. The knowledge of the performance of such rituals was preserved, however, in small and exclusive Brahmin circles, especially in South India. Thus in 1975 the well-known Indologist Frits Staal was able, after long preparations, to have a group of Nambudri brahmins perform the *Agnicayana*, which he filmed. It is fascinating to watch the brahmins prepare the place for the sacrifice, mould and fire the bricks, lay the fire-altar, go through the extensive ceremonies lasting several days, and in the end, burn down the entire structure. Staal believed that it might have been the last chance to observe such a sacrifice, since the required specialists were rapidly dying out. However, in the last decade or so, a remarkable revival of vedic ritual seems to be taking place in India. In many places one can now see vedic sacrifices being performed, and the people involved in the rituals must be quite numerous again. Not only did a nineteenth-century revivalist movement, the Ārya Samāj, encourage the re-introduction of vedic ritual – in their own worship the fire-sacrifice is the only ritual permitted – but other Hindu revivalist groups are now also actively promoting vedic ritual as a means to underscore the basic unity of Hinduism as built on the foundation of the Vedas.

Suggested further reading

Staal, Frits. *Agni: The Vedic Ritual of the Fire Altar.* 2 vols. University of California Press: Berkeley, 1983.

—— *The Science of Ritual.* Deccan Institute: Poona, 1982.

Stevenson, M. *The Rites of the Twiceborn.* Oxford University Press: Oxford, 1920.

Strickmann, M. (ed.). *Classical Asian Rituals and the Theory of Ritual.* Springer: Berlin, 1986.

Part II
The Hindu Religions

The sheer number and size of Hindu temples, which are visited by huge crowds and in which images of gods are worshipped in elaborate rituals, will amaze any visitor to today's India. Vedic tradition continues to form the basis of much that is important in the Hindu's life, but it is the luxuriant mythology and ritual of the *Purāṇas* that is in the foreground of religious Hinduism today. While vedic ritual impresses by its meticulousness and complexity of detail, puranic religions surprise by their exuberance and seemingly limitless imagination. If we had to be careful to generalize in the case of vedic tradition because of the numerous local variants, we would have to preface any statement about puranic Hinduism with a number of disclaimers: the very sources from which it draws its beliefs and practices are so numerous and so heterogeneous that any attempt to come to general conclusions is doomed to failure. In addition, individual Hindus are largely free to interpret these sources in whatever way they please; and that is exactly what they do. The kind of Hinduism that is articulated in the *Purāṇas* makes much of individual revelations of deities in dreams and visions, gives great importance to personalities considered manifestations of a deity, and is as important for the economy as for the spirituality of India. The following chapters will identify the major sources of Hinduism and introduce three 'mainstream' Hindu religions, viz. Vaiśṇavism, Śaivism and Śāktism, leaving out the numerous smaller religious communities and the hundreds of monastic orders that follow their own inspirations.

Tirupati shrine, Andhra Pradesh

5

The heart of Hinduism

An often-quoted verse says: '*Śruti* and *Smṛti* are the two eyes of *Dharma*, but the *Purāṇa* is its heart – on no other foundation does it rest but on these three.' There is no doubt that the religion represented by the *Purāṇas* is the one the makes Hinduism what it is. Together with the *Purāṇas* we have to consider the two Great Epics, the *Mahābhārata* and the *Rāmāyaṇa*, collectively called *Itihāsa* ('history'), that play a considerable role in the religious imagination of Hindus. One small section of the *Mahābhārata*, the *Bhagavadgītā*, has achieved an extraordinarily important position: it is treated by many Hindus as the epitome of their faith and is the focus of innumerable lectures and the subject of countless books. Collectively this literature is the main source for Hinduism as it is practised today by hundreds of millions of Hindus, and is referred to as authoritative by hundreds of thousands of religious teachers. Considering the sheer mass of writings covered by it, the following can make no more than an attempt briefly to describe its general character and to provide some detail.

The *Purāṇas*: the Bibles of Hinduism

The *Purāṇas* (literally 'old (books)'), occupy as central a role in the faith of most Hindus as does the Bible for the followers of Judaism and Christianity. According to the *Purāṇas*' own account, Brahmā, the creator, uttered them before all scriptures; only later did he communicate the *Vedas* to humankind. Consequently many Hindus accord the status of *śruti*, divine revelation, to the *Purāṇas* of their choice. There are altogether eighteen so-called *Mahāpurāṇas* ('Great Puranas'), and a very large number of so-called *Upapurāṇas* ('lesser' Puranas). The *Mahāpurāṇas* have been divided into Vaiṣṇava, Śaiva, and Śakta Purāṇas, extolling respectively Viṣṇu, Śiva or Devī as Supreme Being. The *Upapurāṇas*, in addition to these, also extol Sūrya, the sun, Gaṇeśa, the elephant-headed son of Śiva and Pārvatī, or some lesser-known deity.

The *Purāṇas* deal with the creation of the universe and its dissolution at the end of time, the description of the world-ages and genealogies of sages and teachers, stories of the salvific deeds of God, and many other subjects, including codes of ethics, the four aims of life, religious observances, places of pilgrimage, rituals and descriptions of heavens and hells. They are inexhaustible storehouses of all kinds of information for anyone interested in Hinduism. Since virtually all of them have been translated into English, it is quite easy to get access to this 'heart of Hinduism' without knowing Sanskrit, the original language in which they were written.

Many questions regarding the age and origin of the *Purāṇas*, their authorship and the authenticity of available texts are still unanswered. Because of their mythological and religious character, Western scholarship originally bypassed the *Purāṇas*, and only relatively recently has a major effort been made to study them seriously. While the claim made by the *Purāṇas* that they antedate the Vedas cannot be substantiated, the possibility that an early form of the *Purāṇas* is as old as the Veda cannot be rejected out of hand. The term *Purāṇa*, perhaps not yet in today's sense, is already found in the *Atharva Veda*, the *Śatapatha Brāhmana*, the *Bṛhadāraṇyaka-Upaniṣad* and other vedic literature. It is possible that the *Purāṇas* arose out of narratives by which the non-officiating participants in vedic sacrifices were entertained. Vedic *yajñas* were long drawn-out rituals in which the majority of participants were mere passive onlookers. To keep them occupied, bards regaled them with stories which later coalesced into the *Purāṇas*. Their multiple origin would explain the lack of uniformity and the absence of an original text that could be used as point of reference. The existing printed editions, no doubt based on manuscripts, show great variation in length and content. Assuming that the beginnings of the *Purāṇas* go back to the vedic age, since there was no fixation of the text as in the case of the Vedas, later centuries kept adding to and changing them. The texts underlying present-day editions were fixed only between *c*. 400 CE and 1000 CE. Some *Purāṇas* mention Muslim rulers. Although they present this information as prophecy of things to come, we must assume that it was added after the advent of Islam in India, i.e. after 900 CE. Some scholars speculate that originally there existed an *Ur-Purāṇa*, a kind of model that was copied and adapted by later authors. They consider the extant *Vāyu-Purāṇa*, one of the shorter of such texts, to be closest to it, since it conforms best to the schema of the ideal content of a *Purāṇa*.

Purāṇas represent the scriptures of Vaiṣṇavism, Śaivism and Śaktism, and their frequently explicitly sectarian presentation of Hinduism does not shy away from denigrating and vilifying other beliefs and practices. They insist on exclusively worshipping the particular deity which they make the centre of their presentation, and attribute salvific effects only to their own sectarian practices. They reflect very closely the attitudes of the average Hindu today and they continue to mould Hinduism more than any other source. They are available in many vernacular versions and are still widely read, and also publicly recited. They promise rich and instant rewards for reading or preserving them and make it easy for their adherents to embark on the way to bliss and salvation.

Among the Vaiśṇava Purāṇas the *Viṣṇupurāṇa* and the *Bhāgavatam* (not to be confused with the much smaller *Bhagavadgītā*) are the most popular. The *Viṣṇupurāṇa* contains, besides the description of the creation and dissolution of the universe, the basic Viṣṇu mythology and stories of great devotees of Viṣṇu like Prahlāda, who was saved from the persecutions of his unbelieving father by an intervention of

Viṣṇu appearing as *Nāra-sinha*, the man-lion. The *Bhāgavatam*, one of the larger *Purāṇas*, has become famous for its extensive treatment of Kṛṣṇa and his exploits. Both the *Viṣṇupurāṇa* and the *Bhāgavatam* are treated by their adherents as direct revelation from Viṣṇu.

Śaivas possess in the *Śivapurāṇa*, the *Liṅgapurāṇa* and the very voluminous *Skandhapurāṇa* rich sources of Śiva mythology.

Similarly, the Śaktas consider the *Devīpurāṇa* and the *Mārkandeyapurāṇa* authoritative texts authenticating their tradition. A small section of the latter, the so-called *Devīmāhātmya*, describing the victory of the Goddess over the demon Mahiṣāsura, is recited by millions every year at the time of the great Durgā festival. It promises to the reader salvation from all adversity.

The major Hindu communities, Vaiṣṇavas, Śaivas and Śāktas, base their teachings and rituals largely on their respective *Purāṇas*. Some detail of these will be offered in the next chapters.

The *Mahābhārata*: the great epic of India

Peter Brooks' nine-hour dramatic recreation of the *Mahābhārata* has made millions in the West familiar with the great figures and themes of this largest epic of all, and has also convinced them of the powerful imagination of its creators. The text of the *Mahābhārata*, now available in a twenty-one-volume critical edition and in several English translations, has the character more of an encyclopedia than of a single piece of literature. It says about itself that 'what is in the *Mahābhārata* may be found elsewhere too, but what is not found there, is found nowhere'. Probably beginning as a heroic tale about the fratricidal battle between the Pāṇḍavas and the Kauravas, it was expanded by the addition of all kinds of extraneous materials, till it reached its present huge proportion of 100,000 *ślokas* (couplets), or eight times the *Iliad* and the *Odyssey*, the largest European epics, put together. The original story now occupies less than a fifth of the *Mahābhārata*, which has become a major source for traditional ethical and practical wisdom of life.

The plot of the Bhārata story can be sketched out in a few paragraphs: it begins with the two sons of King Vicitravīrya – Dhṛtarāṣṭra and Pāṇḍu. Dhṛtarāṣṭra, the elder, is to succeed his father to the throne. However, being born blind, he is considered unable to exercise kingship, and thus his younger brother Pāṇḍu is enthroned. Pāṇḍu dies after a short reign, leaving behind five sons, all minors. Blind Dhṛtarāṣṭra takes over as king. His hundred sons, the Kauravas, grow up together with the Pāṇḍavas, the five sons of his deceased brother Pāṇḍu. Reaching adulthood, Duryodhana, the eldest son of Dhṛtarāṣṭra, claims the throne for himself and tries to eliminate the Pāṇḍavas through a series of criminal plots. He succeeds in exiling the five brothers together with their common wife Draupadī. While Duryodhana believes that he has freed himself of them for good, the Pāṇḍavas win allies and challenge Duryodhana to a battle. In order to avoid a war, old king Dhṛtarāṣṭra divides the kingdom, giving one half to his sons and one half to the Pāṇḍava brothers. The situation remains tense.

A minor incident provides the spark for a catastrophe. Duryodhana, now king at Hastināpūra, a city sixty miles from Delhi, while visiting his cousin Yudhiṣṭhira, king at Indraprāṣṭa, identified with Old Delhi, slips and falls into a pond. Draupadī breaks out in uncontrolled laughter. Duryodhana, feeling he has lost face, challenges Yudhiṣṭhira to a game of dice where the winner takes all. Yudhiṣṭhira, a passionate gambler, loses everything: his kingdom, his army, his brothers, and finally Draupadī, the Pāndava brothers' common wife. She refuses to appear before Duryodhana but is rudely pulled in, and an attempt made to disrobe her. Bhīma, one of the Pāndavas, takes a terrible oath: he vows not to rest till he had killed Duryodhana and drunk his blood.

Blind old Dhṛtarāṣṭra intervenes again. Duryodhana settles for a dangerous compromise. Instead of returning the lost half of the kingdom to the Pāndavas, he agrees to a second round of dice: the loser will have to go into exile in the jungle for twelve years, remain incognito for another year, and only then be allowed to regain his kingdom. Should he be found out during the thirteenth year, he will have to endure exile for a further twelve-year period. The Pāndavas lose the game again and leave for their forest exile. They manage to remain undiscovered during the thirteenth year, and reclaim their kingdom. Yet since Duryodhana refuses to honour the previous deal, both parties prepare for an all-out war to decide the question of succession.

The war, considered by Hindus the bloodiest and most catastrophic in their entire history, lasts for eighteen days. Millions of people die. The Pāndavas, not always following the rules of chivalrous warfare, emerge as winners. Their number is terribly decimated, and instead of rejoicing over their victory and taking possession of their kingdom they start on a last pilgrimage into the Himalayas. All of them die and the author of the last part of the *Mahābhārata* muses on the futility of a war that seemed so utterly pointless, yet appeared to have been predestined.

Besides the sometimes frighteningly realistic description of the brutality of war, the *Mahābhārata*, even in the sections dealing with the strife between the two clans, contains beautiful stories relating to the Pāndavas' wanderings through the forest, moral lessons and entertaining passages – riddles, myths and a kind of tourist guide through the *āśrams* in the forests of India. It has provided the plots for a great many dramas written by playwrights in later times and has also been kept alive through regular performances by bands of itinerant bards. The names of the heroes and heroines of the *Mahābhārata* are still given to many Indians today and one can see that the great epic of India has remained much more alive through the several thousand years of its existence than any of the great European epics of a later age. The recent multi-part television series *Mahābhārata* was avidly watched by millions of Indians, who see in it a document of the heroic lives of their forebears.

The *Ramāyāna*: the Hindus' favourite book

If television audiences are a gauge of popularity, nothing in recent years has beaten the dramatization of the *Rāmāyana*. Every Sunday morning, when an episode was broadcast, millions were glued to their television sets. In many towns and villages life came to a standstill while everyone watched the progress of the drama of Rāma and Sītā. For most Hindus it was not just watching a television play, but became a form of worship. The attention paid to the contemporary re-enactment of the ancient epic had a variety of reasons. It certainly revealed the enduring attraction which this most ancient of India's poetic creations possesses.

The *Rāmāyana* is ascribed to the poet Vālmīki, who according to tradition lived around 2200 BCE in the area around Ayodhyā, in today's Uttar Pradesh. According to legend, he had been converted from a life of brigandry to the worship of Rāma. He did such intense penance, sitting motionless in one place, that termites, in Sanskrit *vālmīkas*, built a hill around him, so that only his eyes remained visible. That is why he is called Vālmīki. The *Rāmāyana* is shorter and more unified than the *Mahābhārata*. While also containing lyrical descriptions of bucolic scenes and exhortations of a moral nature, it tells in its main body the story of Rāma, the ideal king, and his exploits.

Rāma was the son of king Daśaratha and queen Kauś alyā, one of his three wives. Rāma, together with his half-brothers, received the education appropriate for a prince and future ruler. His marriage to Sītā, daughter of king Janaka of Videha, was a major event: Rāma had been the only one of Sītā's many suitors who passed the test by lifting the bow of Rudra, which was in the king's possession. Ramā and Sītā spent a brief, happy time together in Ayodhyā, liked by all the people. Daśaratha, ready to retire, intended to have Rāma crowned king. Extensive preparations were made. However, the night before the installation ceremony Kaikeyī, another one of Daśaratha's wives, forced the king to cancel the event. Kaikeyī's maid-servant, the hunchback Mantharā, had insinuated that Rāma, after being made king, would kill his potential rivals, including his half-brother Bharata, Kaikeyī's only son. Given past practice at royal courts, this did not sound implausible.

Kaikeyī had to do everything to save her son. She remembered that on some earlier occasion when she had saved Daśaratha's life after a battle, the king had promised her to fulfil any two wishes she might utter at any time. Kaikeyī now reminded him of the promise and demanded that Bharata, her own son, be made king and Rāma be sent into exile. Daśaratha, according to the code of honour of a nobleman, had to keep his word. Rāma agreed and prepared to leave for exile in the forest. His wife Sītā, in spite of being warned of the hardships to be encountered, decided to accompany him. So did Lakṣmaṇa, another one of Rāma's half-brothers.

The fourteen years which Rāma, Sītā and Lakṣmaṇa spent in the forest were filled with many incidents and adventures. The most important was the abduction of Sītā by Rāvaṇa, the demon-king of Laṅkā. It forms an epic within the epic and is the subject of many popular plays. After much anxiety and uncertainty Rāma, with the help of an army of monkeys led by Hanuman, their general, who had befriended him, was able to take Lanka by storm. Sītā was recovered and restored to Rāma. The years of forest exile over, Rāma and Sītā triumphantly re-entered Ayodhyā, and Bharata handed over his rulership to Rāma, whom he had always considered the rightful king. However, what could have been a happy end turned into tragedy: disturbed by public comments on Sītā's lengthy captivity by Rāvaṇa, Rāma asked her to undergo a fire ordeal to prove her innocence. Sītā passed the test but was nevertheless sent into exile. After many years she returned with her two sons whom she handed over to Rāma, took a final oath of purification and was swallowed up by the earth.

The *Rāmāyaṇa* ends with Rāma, his brothers and all the citizens of Ayodhyā approaching the river Sarayu, at whose banks the royal city was located. There Rāma merged with the body of Viṣṇu, thus demonstrating his divine origin, and disappearing from earth.

The poetic language of the *Rāmāyaṇa*, as well as the characters it presents, have made it the favourite book of Hindus. It has been re-created in many Indian vernaculars and is performed in thousands of towns and villages every year during the autumnal Dassehra festival cycle. The *Rāmāyaṇa* itself contains the prophecy that it will be read in the country of Bhārata as long as its rivers flow and its mountains stand. Hindu India certainly would not be what it is without it and, as recent Western performances of scenes from the *Rāmāyaṇa* have proved, the adventures of Rāma and Sītā can move the hearts of people all over the world.

The *Bhagavadgītā*

It is probably safe to say that the Hindu book best known all the world over is the *Bhagavadgītā*, 'The Song of the Lord'. Since its first translation into English in 1785 it has been rendered into hundreds of languages and printed in millions of copies. Many treat it as a compendium of Hinduism, and many Hindus know it by heart. Its chapters are regularly chanted at worship services, and it is lectured on every day by countless preachers.

The text itself forms a section of eighteen chapters in the sixth book of the *Mahābhārata* and stands at the crucial juncture of the beginning of the great battle between the Pāṇḍavas and the Kauravas. The *Gītā* proper is set into a double frame: the listener is informed about the impending debacle. Dhṛtarāṣṭra, the blind old King-father, sits on the sidelines and asks Sanjaya, his *sūta* – charioteer and reporter in one – to tell him about the goings on. Within the narrative itself, the dialogues between Arjuna, the leader of the Pāṇḍavas, and Kṛṣṇa, who acts as his charioteer, occupy the centre stage.

At the heart of the *Gītā* is an ethical dilemma: Arjuna, ready to decide the question of succession to Dhṛtarāṣṭra's kingdom by a war, as suggested by the hostile Kauravas, is having second thoughts: the 'enemy' whom he is facing consists of blood-relations, former teachers, members of his own family. According to the traditional ethic of warriors, internecine warfare brings about the downfall of the family and punishment in hell. Arjuna is therefore resolved to forgo his kingdom in order to preserve his peace of mind. He is prepared to become a recluse and a beggar rather than a murderer of his own family. Kṛṣṇa disagrees. He reminds him of his duty as a warrior, suggests that people will consider him a coward, and points out that as a *kṣatriya* he could not opt out by becoming a *saṁnyāsi*, a stage of life open only to the *brahmin*. 'You have to fight,' he tells him.

The discussion goes back and forth, Arjuna finding problems with Kṛṣṇa's arguments proffered in favour of war, until finally Kṛṣṇa reveals himself as God in a grandiose vision as the all-encompassing universe. There Arjuna sees the whole world-spectacle unfolding before himself: the great battle, which he is dreading, is part of it – already a fact, not a future option. Shaken, he understands that all life is but a fragment of an eternal and immutable world-plan established by God, and that he is to play the part allotted to him by his birth into a *kṣatriya* clan, regardless of his own feelings or preferences.

Kṛṣṇa not only reveals to Arjuna his own divine nature and the fact that he has appeared in human form many times before, but also instructs him about the indestructible self that he himself possesses, which is capable of changing bodies like garments. Birth and death are illusory from the standpoint of the eternal self, the real self – there is no question of killing or being killed. The self is not touched by what happens to the body. Nor is there any question of sin or guilt in carrying out one's duty: sin arises only from evil intentions. If Arjuna did rid himself of all feelings of hatred, greed and desire, and acted only out of a sense of duty, his actions would not bring about *karma*: desireless action, *niṣkāma karma*, is the solution to Arjuna's dilemma.

DO YOUR WORK

Your work is your responsibility, not its result.
Never let the fruits of your actions be your motive,
Nor give in to inaction.

Set firmly in yourself do your work, not attached to anything,
Remain evenminded in success and in failure;
Evenmindedness is true yoga.

Mere activity is inferior to insight;
Gain insight!
To be pitied are those who look for the fruit of their deeds.

One who has reached insight is beyond good and evil.
The wise who have gained insight renounce the fruit of their work.
Freed from the bonds of rebirth, they reach the sorrowless state.

Bhagavadgītā II, 47–51

In addition to this central message – one that is taken very seriously also by contemporary Hindus, who accept the *Gītā's* position that a person is only responsible for carrying out his duty and not for the consequences of so doing – the *Gītā* deals with many other important religious issues. Classical Hindu authors, beginning with the eighth-century philosopher Śaṅkara, have extensively commented on the *Bhagavadgītā*, thus making of it a core text in the philosophical schools of India. The lengthy commentaries and their not infrequent disagreements should caution us not to consider the *Gītā* an easy book, in spite of its popularity. It requires lengthy study and searching inquiry before it yields some of its deeper insights.

The 'heart of Hinduism' – the *Purāṇas*, the Epics, and especially the *Bhagavadgītā* – is alive in today's India and beating vigorously.

Hindu jāgaran, the awakening of Hinduism in our age, is largely founded on this core of popular texts. The fact that they have grown over many centuries, and were performed and interpreted in ever new ways throughout the ages, has kept them alive and full of meaning for every new generation of Hindus. To learn what Hinduism means to Hindus, there is no better way than to read and study the Epics and the *Purāṇas* and their modern renderings.

Suggested further reading

Pusalker, A. D. *Studies in Epics and Puranas of India*. Bharatiya Vidya Bhavan: Bombay, 1955.

Rocher, Ludo. *The Puranas*. Vol. 2, fasc. 3 of *History of Indian Literature*. Harassowitz: Wiesbaden, 1986.

van Nooten, B. A. *The Mahabharata*, Twayne: New York, 1971.

Winternitz, Moritz. *The Popular Epics and the Puranas*. Vol. 1 part 2 of *A History of Indian Literature*. University of Calcutta: Calcutta, 1963.

6

Lord Viṣṇu and his devotees

The largest community within the family of religions called Hinduism worships the Supreme under the name of Viṣṇu, 'the All-pervader'. The Vaiṣṇavas, as they are called, are divided into many smaller communities, often focusing their devotion on one of the *avatras*, the visible manifestations of Viṣṇu. Besides age-old local traditions that differ from one place to the next, there are historic developments initiated by well-known personalities that have created new branches differing from each other in philosophy, ritual or doctrine.

Lord Viṣṇu

Among the many deities (*devatās*) invoked in the *Ṛgveda* there is Viṣṇu, described as the younger brother of Indra, the vedic chief deity. Viṣṇu is associated with the sun and its movement across the sky. The oldest known myth is that of *Viṣṇu trivikrama*, 'Viṣṇu who takes the three steps'. The story appears in many sources and was later associated with the legend of the *Vāmana avatāra*, the 'dwarf descent'. Bali, a demon world-ruler, invited gods and kings to celebrate a great sacrifice. Every one of the guests could express a wish which the host would instantly fulfil. Viṣṇu, who had appeared as a dwarf, asked only for a small piece of land – as much as he could cover with three strides. Bali encouraged him to ask for a larger gift, something worthy of a world ruler. The dwarf insisted

Viṣṇu Sanctuary, Vrindāban, Uttar Pradesh

on his wish. Bali gave in. And before his eyes the dwarf began to grow to huge dimensions. His first step covered the entire earth. The second step reached the sun, and there was no more room for a third step. So Bali offered his head for Viṣṇu's foot to rest on, thus acknowledging his supremacy.

Another vedic myth, found in the famous *Puruṣasūkta* of the *Ṛigveda*, has become the basis of the later Vaiṣṇava doctrine of the universe as God's body. In it all beings are described as originating from the body of a primordial being, everything in this world being but a transformation of his body.

A PRAYER TO VIṢṆU

Lord, you dwell in everything, you are everything, you take all forms and you are the origin of everything. You are the Self of all.

You, the Self of all beings, the Lord of all creation, you are the source of all that exists. You know everybody's desire.

Salutations to you, the omnipresent, who are inseparably linked with the universe. You are the first object of all meditation.

From *Viṣṇupurāṇa* Ch. XII

The major sources, however, for Viṣṇu theology are the aforementioned *Purāṇas* and the *Saṁhitās*, a class of voluminous writings detailing Viṣṇu worship and its rationale. Among the *Purāṇas*, the *Viṣṇupurāṇa*, in its present form dating from the fifth century CE, occupies a special place. For Vaiṣnavas it is *śruti*, a revealed text. It describes the creation of the universe by Viṣṇu as Brahmā and the revelation of the Vedas through Viṣṇu. Viṣṇu's power as saviour of his devotees is illustrated in the famous story of Prahlāda, which is often enacted in popular plays.

Prahlāda was the son of the powerful demon king Hiraṇyakaśipu, who considered himself the greatest. Sending his son away for schooling, he wanted to find out what he had learned.

Prahlāda told him he had learned that Viṣṇu was the greatest god, all-powerful and omnipresent. Hiraṇyakaśipu, displeased, changed teachers. Re-examining his son after further years of training, he found that Prahladā's answer was unchanged. After several futile attempts to re-educate his son, Hiraṇyakaśipu decided to kill him. He had him submerged, poisoned, thrown from high cliffs – but by the grace of Viṣṇu Prahlāda survived it all, continuing to extol Viṣṇu's greatness. Hiraṇyakaśipu, beside himself with fury, drew his sword, yelling at Prahlāda: 'Tell your Viṣṇu to save you now from my sword, if he can!' Kicking a column in his palace, Hiraṇyakaśipu shouted: 'Your Viṣṇu will be of as little help to you as this piece of stone.' But lo and behold, out of the column appeared Viṣṇu in the shape of Nārasinha, half man and half lion, devouring Hiraṇyakaśipu and thus saving his devotee Prahlāda. For the pious Vaiṣṇava the Prahlāda story is the warrant for Viṣṇu's salvific will and power: Viṣṇu will save his devotees from all dangers, finally rewarding them with eternal bliss in his heaven.

Usually Viṣṇu is represented together with his consort Śri or Lakṣmī, 'Good Fortune' or 'Wealth'. Mediaeval theologians like Rāmānuja developed quite an extensive theology of the goddess as well, attributing to her mediatorship between Viṣṇu and his devotees and channelling Viṣṇu's grace to them. The figure of Viṣṇu shows a small mark on the left side of his chest – the *Śrīvatsa*, the sign of the constant presence of Viṣṇu's divine consort. Beautiful hymns praise her as mother of the universe and as saviour from distress.

Viṣṇu *avatāras*

Today's Vaiṣṇavism is strongly shaped by the devotion to *avatāras*, 'descents' of Viṣṇu into bodily forms. The most common tradition speaks of ten such *avatāras*:

- *Matsya* – fish
- *Kūrma* – tortoise
- *Varāha* – boar
- *Nārasinha* – man-lion
- *Vāmana* – dwarf
- *Paraśurāma* – Rāma with the battle-ax
- *Rāma*
- *Kṛṣṇa*
- *Buddha*
- *Kalki*, who brings about the end of the aeon.

Many texts mention twenty-two or thirty-six or state that Viṣṇu's *avatāras* are infinite in number. Considering the facility with which Hindus at all times have recognized important personages as embodiments of divinities, the latter option is quite plausible.

The Rāma and Kṛṣṇa *avatāras* are by far the most popular ones, and an immense literature has developed over the centuries, detailing their exploits and celebrating their achievements. The earlier mentioned *Rāmāyaṇa* and its many vernacular re-creations, especially Tulsidas' Hindi *Rāmcaritmanas*, are holy books for Rāma worshippers, as the *Bhagavadgītā* and the *Bhāgavata Purāṇa* are for the devotees of Kṛṣṇa. Both groups have developed a large number of religious orders, each with its own theology and ritual. While they do have a great deal in common, the differences between them – at least from the standpoint of the adherents of each group – are large enough to create tension and occasional outbreaks of hostility among them.

The Rāma story, as told by Vālmīki in the Sanskrit *Rāmāyaṇa*, has already been briefly dealt with. Rāma and Sītā were probably celebrated locally long before they were divinized into *avatāras*. Ayodhyā, the reputed residence of Rāma, has become the major pilgrimage centre for Rāma devotees. Several thousand members of the Rāmānandi order have taken up permanent residence there, and millions come every year to visit the places connected with

Rāma's and Sītā's lives. Ayodhyā became the centre of Hindu political agitations that led, in December 1992, to the demolition of an (unused) mosque which had been built on the traditional birthplace of Rāma after a centuries-old Hindu temple had been razed to the ground by Babur, a Moghul ruler. Rāma, as *dharma-rāja*, the King of Righteousness, has become the focus for Hindu political parties, and his rule, in which justice and prosperity prevailed, has become the model for India's renewal.

The most popular *avatāra*, however, is doubtlessly Kṛṣṇa, the Black One, also called Śyāma, whom many hold to be identical with, and not just a partial manifestation of, the Supreme. Besides the *Bhagavadgītā*, in which Kṛṣṇa appears as teacher and as embodiment of *dharma*, there is the *Bhāgavata Purāṇa* (also called the *Bhāgavatam*) containing the stories of Kṛṣṇa's infancy and youth, which have become immensely popular. They have been elaborated by some of the greatest poets of India, made into hugely entertaining plays, and have provided the basis for sophisticated theologies, an inspiration for the most beautiful paintings and sculptures as well as music and dance.

The question of the historicity of Kṛṣṇa and the identity of the various aspects that appear in his worship today is being studied seriously by Indian scholars, and recent explorations of Dvārakā, the reputed capital of Kṛṣṇa, have revealed an extensive city, largely submerged in the Arabian Sea, dating back to *c.* 1650 BCE. Sculptures showing Kṛṣṇa's foster-mother Yaśodā with the Divine Child have been found in and around Mathurā, dating back to the second century BCE. Early Western visitors to India reported the popularity of the worship of Kṛṣṇa, whom the Greeks identified with Heracles. There is no doubt that most of the mediaeval Hindu revival movements were inspired by Kṛṣṇa's exploits as narrated by the tenth-century *Bhāgavatam*. Today, the devotees of Kṛṣṇa far outnumber all others.

As Viṣṇu is always accompanied by Śrī or Lakṣmī, so Viṣṇu's *avatāras* (descents) are accompanied by female counterparts of

Śrī: Sītā is Rāma's faithful wife and Rādhā is Kṛṣṇa's eternal companion. While Rāma devotion celebrates the virtues of the married couple Rāma and Sītā, Kṛṣṇa worship appears to centre on passionate love outside marriage. Many complicated interpretations of the *Bhāgavatam*, a revealed text for Kṛṣṇa worshippers, have been produced to bring the Rādhā-Kṛṣṇa romance in line with accepted Hindu moral standards. The most frequent explanation is that Rādhā symbolizes the soul and is not to be understood as a real woman, and that the erotically couched Rādhā-Kṛṣṇa stories are meant to inspire love of God by way of sublimation and transcendence of the most intense human feeling.

Image worship and its rationale

Much of Hinduism, and especially Vaiṣṇavism, is intimately connected with images and image-worship. Images, in the understanding of Hindus, are not mere artistic representations of otherwise abstract theological notions, but are God's physical presence. According to Pāñcarātra doctrine, which forms the basis of Vaiṣṇava theology, the Supreme Viṣṇu, who in his transcendent nature is inaccessible to humans, made himself successively available by descending first into super-human spiritual beings called *vyūhas*, then into a number of corporeal *avatāras*, further descending into every human heart as an inner presence, called *antaryāmin*, 'the ruler within', and finally materializing as *ārcāvatāra*. God's visible presence in an image made of stone or metal. The image, called *mūrti* (embodiment), is of central importance in Vaiṣṇavism. Some images are found, usually through revelation in dreams, and are believed to contain Viṣṇu's presence. Others are made by artists, according to specifications laid down in the texts of *śilpa-śāstra*, the Hindu handbooks of art and architecture. Through an elaborate consecration ceremony performed by an authorized person, the lifeless material image is transformed into a *mūrti*, a presence of

Viṣṇu, and the believers come to have *darśan*, to see God. The *mūrti* is the centre of a temple, the focus of all worship, and the fame of a temple depends on the power of a *mūrti*, its reputation for granting wishes and performing miracles. Apart from anthropomorphic figures, Vaiṣṇavas consider the *tulasī*-plant (sacred basil) and the *śālagrāma*, a round stone found in the Gandak river in Nepal, as embodiments of Viṣṇu. Every Vaiṣṇava family keeps a *tulasī* plant in a pot, and some *śālagrāmas* in the house.

An elaborate ritual is required of Vaiṣṇavas in order to do justice to God's condescension in making himself available in the form of an image. The *mūrti* is treated like an honoured royal guest. Early in the morning it is awakened through clapping of hands and playing of soft music; it is washed, dressed, garlanded. Incense is burned before it and it is offered a breakfast. Hymns are recited for it, usually with the accompaniment of cymbals. In homes these rituals are usually performed on a smaller scale; in temples there may be loud shouting of the god's names, singing and dancing before the image, and a solemn distribution of *prasāda*, the leftovers of the food offered to the deity, which is consumed by the worshippers like a sacrament, or taken home to be shared with those who did not attend temple-service. There is usually an offering at noon and in the evening, when the image is laid to rest. The most conspicuous ceremony at night is *āratī*, the waving of lights before the image. After the flame has been brought back to the worshippers, they each touch it and bring their hands up to their foreheads to share the blessing. At particular times during the year elaborate festivals are celebrated, each revolving around the image. Since the *mūrti* is legally the owner of the temple and all that belongs to it, be it buildings or tracts of land, it is at certain occasions taken out and shown its possessions. At the beginning of the hot season in many places the image is taken in procession on a sometimes many-storeyed chariot to a cooler location, and conducted back to the main temple at the beginning of the rains.

There are many local customs and variants in the ritual of image worship, but its centrality is unquestioned. Hindus do believe that God is present in the image, and they consider it important to visit the *mūrtis* of famous places in the expectation of material and spiritual benefits. The highest act of devotion, however, is to build a house for such a *Mūrti*, to have a temple constructed according to the elaborate traditional rules. India is full of old temples, big and small, but in the last few decades thousands of new temples were built in towns and cities. Many of these are beautiful palaces with all modern amenities, which attract large masses of worshippers. Industrialists and other affluent citizens of India also immortalize themselves in our time by supporting the construction of new temples, which nowadays often also contain rooms for congregational worship.

Vaiṣṇava theology

Since time immemorial Hindus have attempted to gain knowledge of the divine, to systematize their insights and to propagate their findings. Some of the late *Upaniṣads*, such as the *Avyakta* or the *Gopāla Upaniṣads*, provide a systematics of Vaiṣṇava doctrines which were further elaborated by mediaeval thinkers. When Bādarāyaṇa's *Brahmasūtras* became universally accepted as a compendium of vedantic thought, each branch of Hinduism worked out its own commentary on that work in order to show its orthodoxy, and in the process also to clarify its own doctrinal position. Since Hinduism did not develop from one common centre and never had a central magisterium, individual scholars had to undertake in their own time the task of reconciling different and often contradictory interpretations that had developed over the centuries. In the case of Vaiṣṇavism, the vedic, sanskritic tradition, the Purāṇas and the Epics, the many local histories and the exuberant, spontaneous, vernacular outpourings of mystics and poets all had to be brought together when, in the ninth century, the *ācāryas* of

Śrīraṅgam, a temple-city in South India and an ancient centre of Viṣṇu worship, attempted to offer a new systematics of Hinduism. This was seen as important not only in the face of non-Hindu religions like Buddhism and Jainism, which were still strong in some places, but also in view of the widely accepted interpretation of Hinduism by Śaṅkara in the eighth century. This the Vaiṣṇavas believed to be mistaken because it left out much that was central to them, such as image worship and the notion of the ultimate as a person different from individual human selves. Taking a wider view of 'revealed scriptures' than Śaṅkara, the Śrīraṅgam pontiffs, of whom Rāmānuja (1017–1137 CE) was the greatest, based their presentation of Hinduism not only on Upaniṣadic texts, as Śaṅkara had done, but included among their theological sources the whole *Veda*, the epics, the *Viṣṇu Purāṇa*, the hymns of the Āḷvārs (a group of Tamil poet-mystics), and the entire worship tradition. Understandably the task took a long time, and many loose ends remained. On the whole, however, it was a success, and later developments in Vaiṣṇavism built upon it.

From the twelfth century onwards huge waves of emotionally charged Vaiṣṇava devotion swept especially through northern India. Ancient centres connected with the lives of Rāma and Kṛṣṇa, like Ayodhyā and Vṛndāban, were rediscovered and revived. New religious orders and schools developed within Vaiṣṇavism, under the leadership of major figures like Vallabha and Caitanya, who attracted millions of followers. The new Vaiṣṇavism often broke through the traditional barriers of caste and sex. Among its accepted poet-saints were women like Āṇḍāl and Mīrabāī and an outcaste like Rāīdās.

Vaiṣṇava *saṁpradāyas*

Hindu religious practice is shaped by *saṁpradāyas*, often translated as 'sects', but roughly comparable to denominations or churches in the Western context. The founders and the subsequent leaders of each *saṁpradāya* regulate the life of the members, determine the religious routine and demarcate the boundaries for acceptable and unacceptable practices and readings. Normally a Hindu who is religiously active would seek affiliation with, or initiation into, one of these *saṁpradāyas*, most of which maintain centres in major places of pilgrimage.

In the fourteenth century a conference of Vaiṣṇava religious leaders agreed to a structuring of the many Vaiṣṇava *saṁpradāyas* into the so-called *catuḥ saṁpradāya*, affiliating each of them with one of four 'mainstream' *saṁpradāyas*:

- *Śrīvaiṣṇava* (Rāmānuja)
- *Brahmā* (Madhva)
- *Kumāra* (Nimbārka)
- *Rudra* (Viṣṇuswāmi and Vallabha).

All later Vaiṣṇava congregations were to seek affiliation with one of these four in order to be recognized as legitimate. Two major developments, however, the Caitanya and the Śrī *saṁpradāya*, while nominally affiliated with the Brahmā and Rudra *saṁpradāyas*, have become fairly independent and, due to the number of followers, quite influential.

Caitanya (*c.* 1485–1533 CE) especially, as the founder of the Gauḍīya Vaiṣṇava school, which became known in the West as ISKCON (International Society for Kṛṣṇa Consciousness), deserves mention. He was considered by his followers an *avatāra* of both Rādhā and Kṛṣṇa and initiated a strand of Vaiṣṇavism in which emotions played the main role. Building on the traditional Indian *rasa* ('emotions') theory, which underlies Hindu aesthetics, he declared Kṛṣṇa to be the embodiment of all feelings, and the cultivation of emotions the supreme path to God. Using the language of erotic love and celebrating the mystery of the union of Kṛṣṇa and Rādhā through public dancing and singing (*nāgara saṅkīrtan*) he inspired scholars like Jīva and Rūpa Gosvāmi as well as ordinary people, and became the focus of a mass movement in Bengal and beyond. His immediate disciples were responsible for rediscovering and reviving ancient Vṛndāban and making it one of the foremost places of pilgrimage in the whole of India.

Vaiṣṇavism today is a vibrant religion, alive in dozens of different *saṁpradāyas*, adhered to by over 300 million Hindus. Its major centres, like Śrīrangam and Tirupati in South India, Ayodhyā and Mathurā-Vṛndāban in the North, Puri and Māyāpur in the East (to name only some of several hundred), are constantly overflowing with millions of pilgrims, and the major temples resound day and night with the uninterrupted worship through which devotees hope to win the grace of Viṣṇu, the universal Lord.

Suggested further reading

Gonda, Jan. *Aspects of Early Vishnuism*. Motilal Banarsidass: Delhi, 1965.

Hawley, J. S. *Krishna, the Butter Thief*. Princeton University Press: Princeton, 1983.

Macnicol, N. *Indian Theism*. Oxford University Press: London, 1915.

Singer, Milton (ed.). *Krishna: Myths, Rites and Attitudes*. University of Chicago Press: Chicago, 1969.

7

Śiva means grace

The roots of Śaivism are deeply anchored in India's past. Its beginning points to pre-historic times, about which, however, it is impossible to do more than guess. A seal from the Indus civilization shows a horned figure, surrounded by various animals. It has been suggested that this may be a representation of Śiva Paśupati, Śiva the Lord of Animals, a frequently invoked deity of vedic times. Another seal shows a man sitting cross-legged, apparently in deep meditation. The figure has been dubbed Śiva, the Great Yogi. Both designations are still used by Śaivas. Also *liṅgas*, the phallic symbols of Śiva, still widely encountered in today's India, have apparently been found at Harappa and Mohenjo Daro.

Arguably the oldest Śiva myth, the destruction of Dakṣa's sacrifice, suggests a struggle between the followers of Śiva and the representatives of vedic religion. Śaivism was accepted and respected relatively late within vedic tradition. It surely contained elements of indigenous tribal religions and was felt to be alien to the vedic ethos. The Rudra of the *Ṛgveda*, who became identified with Śiva, did not receive his share of offerings at the fire altar: Rudra's portion was deposited outside the village on a crossing, and he was asked to stay away, rather than to approach. His visitations were associated with misfortune and bad luck.

The sources of later Śaivism

In the early middle ages Śaivism became the predominant religion of India, especially in the South. The rulers of some major kingdoms became Śaivites and patronized its representatives.

Saṃbandar, a Saivite saint

Magnificent temples were built in Śiva's honour, and beautiful sculptures made to represent the various forms in which Śiva was believed to have manifested himself. The best known of these motifs is undoubtedly *Naṭarāja*, Śiva as King of Dance. The sources for this 'modern' Śaivism are quite accessible. There are Śaivite sections in the *Mahābhārata*, and Śiva myths are recorded also in the *Rāmāyaṇa*. The *Śvetāśvatara Upaniṣad*, which in Śaivism occupies a role comparable to that of the *Bhagavadgītā* for Vaiṣṇavas, already contains a compendium of Śaivite theology. The Śiva *Purāṇas* and the *Āgamas*, the 'Bibles' of Śaivism, are similar in content and function to the Vaiṣṇava *Purāṇas* and *Saṁhitās*. They recount in great detail the myths on which Śiva's fame rests: they are designed to create confidence in the Great God's power to destroy his enemies and save his devotees. The *Śiva Purānas* and *Āgamas* also give instructions concerning Śiva worship, and promise Śiva's blessings to all who invoke him. There are many parallels between Vaiṣṇavism and Śaivism; one major difference, however, is that Śaivas still perform animal sacrifices, which Vaiṣṇavas abhor.

A further, and perhaps the major source of Śaivism for the population at large are the hymns that were composed by inspired Śaivite poets, which are recited during worship. In these hymns, Śiva is praised and cursed, adored and despised, exalted and ridiculed.

Early on, Śaivism was associated with rigorous, or even excessive, asceticism: Śiva himself is described as the 'Great Yogi' who practised *tapasya*, mortification, to the highest degree. In the fervour of his yogic exercises, Śiva reportedly burned Kāma, the god of love and lust, to ashes, causing a universal withering and wilting of life. Śiva, of course, resurrected Kāma and is also dialectically associated with abandon and the generation of life. The Yoga system as well as the rise of Yogi orders are associated with Śiva. And, as mentioned in connection with Vaiṣṇavism, numerous local Śiva traditions have coalesced into what is acknowledged today as Śaivism. Each of the major Śiva temples, especially in South India, has a local chronicle, enumerating the countless miracles which

A HYMN TO ŚIVA

I worship Śiva in my heart.
He can be known through the Vedas,
He is delightful to the heart,
He has destroyed the three cities,
He is before all time and has three eyes,
He looks majestic with his head of matted locks,
He wears snakes as an ornament and an antelope skin for a dress,
He is the Great God, gracious Lord of Souls,
He is consciousness and bliss,
The companion of Pārvatī.

O Lord of souls!
The one sun that is visible
Takes away the darkness from the earth.
Your splendour surpasses that of a thousand suns.
Why do you not become visible and take away my darkness?
Destroy that night of mine and show yourself to me!

Śaṅkara, *Śivānandalāharī* 3 and 58.

Śiva has performed at that particular place for the benefit of his worshippers. These narratives, in their turn, become vehicles to propagate Śaivism.

Śaiva schools of thought

On the one hand Śaivism puts very great emphasis on largely physical exercises; on the other it has also developed sophisticated systems of theology, admired by students of religion.

Reputedly the oldest text is the *Pāśupatasūtra* ascribed to Lakulin, an *avatāra* (descent) of Śiva. It deals with five subjects that are concerned with the termination of all suffering:

- the condition of bondage in which all humans find themselves
- the Lord and liberator
- the means to liberation
- the appropriate ritual
- final liberation.

The person who is in bondage is called *paśu* (a bovine), being kept in bondage through a noose (*pāśa*) formed of illusion, unrighteousness, attachment and ignorance. The true Lord (*pati*) is Śiva, who with the help of appropriate rituals (*vidhi*), such as repeating sacred formulas (*japa*), meditation, bathing in ashes, singing and laughing, leads the soul to freedom (*mukti*).

Śaiva siddhānta

Śaiva siddhānta, 'the final truth of Śiva', is a school of thought that is followed by many Śaivites today, especially intellectuals. Its teachings are derived from the recognized twenty-eight *Āgamas* and the utterances of the reputed sixty-three *Nāyaṇmārs*. They are systematized in Meykaṇḍa's *Śivajñānabodha*, a text which has received many commentaries by later scholars. According to *Śaiva siddhānta* there are three basic principles:

- the Lord (*pati*)
- the fettered person (*paśu*)
- bondage (*pāśa*).

To gain freedom one has to:

- acquire knowledge (*vidyā*)
- practise rituals (*krīyā*)
- perform austerities (*yoga*)
- live a virtuous life (*cārya*).

Śiva is the supreme reality. He is endowed with independence, purity, self-knowledge, omniscience, freedom from sin, benevolence, omnipotence and blissfulness. The most general way to describe him is as 'being and consciousness' (*sat-cit*). He is immanent in creation; he is male and female and neuter. According to *Śaiva siddhānta*, Śiva cannot have any *avatāras* because this would involve him in a process of becoming, of life and death, which is contrary to his immutable nature. His bodily form is the *guru* who is sent to save souls from the cycle of rebirth (*saṁsāra*). The best characterization of him is: 'Śiva is Love'. The central theme in *Śaiva siddhānta* is the grace of God. Through his form of *Sadaśīva*, often artistically represented, he exercises his fivefold activity of:

- giving grace
- causing delusion
- bringing about destruction
- providing continued existence
- initiating creation.

Human bondage is attributed to three causes:

- *Karma*, which leads to continued existences time after time
- *Māyā*, which comprises the cosmic process of evolution and devolution;
- *Aṇava*, the ego-centred atomistic existence which distorts perception of reality.

Liberation from bondage is an intricate process. Initiation (*dīkṣā*) is the direct means of liberation, but initiation is not possible without knowledge (*vidyā*). Knowledge presupposes *yoga*, which in turn requires ritual acts, and ritual acts are not possible without leading a pure life. Knowledge is of three kinds: knowledge of the soul, the world and the Lord. Only the latter is liberating. The way to acquire it is through the words of the *guru* through whom Śiva appears.

Liberation is the manifestation of the hidden *śivatva*, the concealed God-nature in humans. It is possible to gain liberation while still living in a mortal body (*jīvanmukti*). Those who have become liberated become one with Śiva: their actions, whether considered good or bad by outsiders, no longer affect them. They are beyond good and evil; their deeds are Śiva's deeds.

Śaiva siddhāntins insist that only their teaching is *siddhānta*, i.e. final truth, and that all other doctrines and practices lead at best to one of the six principles (*tattvas*) that are below Śiva.

Kaśmīr Śaivism

Kaśmīr Śaivism, while almost defunct today, developed a great amount of sophisticated philosophical speculation and is being studied by many scholars today. One of the most prolific and original Hindu authors, Abhinavagupta (*c.* 960–1020 CE), was a proponent of this school. The *Śivapurāṇa* gives a lengthy description of this once very important system. It is also called *Pratyābhijñā* ('recognition'), because it begins with the assumption that all reality, including Śiva and Śakti and their union, is mirrored in the human soul, and that liberation consists in recognizing that mirror-image. Śiva is by nature *ānanda*, bliss, and one regains happiness by recognizing one's own Śiva-nature. The followers of this school aim at becoming 'Śiva's slaves'. Since all human unhappiness comes from an illusory restriction of Śiva's nature – the omnipotent, omniscient, eternal, blissful Śiva being reduced to a finite, limited, ignorant and unhappy individual person – one has to strive to 'become Śiva' and regain one's original universal nature.

Viraśaivism

Vīraśaivism, 'heroic Śiva religion', is closely connected with the twelfth-century religious reformer, Basava. Under his inspiration Śaivism developed an active missionary movement. Basava introduced many innovations through which Vīraśaivas distinguish themselves from others. Each member had to wear a Śiva-*liṅga* around his neck at all times, indicating the constant presence of

Śiva. By wearing it the body was transformed into a temple of Śiva. Basava also introduced many social reforms. Thus he abolished caste differences and encouraged entrepreneurship. Among the peculiarities of Vīraśaivism is the custom of burying the dead rather than cremating them as most other Hindus do. The Vīraśaivas today constitute a vigorous community largely centred on Karṇāṭaka.

Śaiva asceticism

From the earliest times Śaivism has been connected with ascetic and yogic practices. Like Śiva himself, some of his followers, by subjecting themselves to rigorous mortifications, attempted to acquire power. The *Daśanāmis*, the ten orders of *samnyāsis* (ascetics), said to have been created by Śaṅkara in the ninth century, are Śaivite. While these are known primarily for their learning and their unflinching quest of the absolute, there are other Śaivite groups that pursue physical, martial training or go to extremes in showing their disdain for 'normal' life. Some, like the *Nāgas*, go completely naked, their bodies besmeared with ashes; others, like the *Aghoris*, live near cremation grounds and are even reported to eat corpses.

Yogis in general are usually Śaivites. Among the many orders of Yogis the *Nāṭhapanthis*, followers of Gorakhnātha, are probably the best known. They are supposed to be constantly on the move. One of their subgroups, the Kānphaṭis ('hole in the ear'), practise a peculiar initiation ceremony: the guru pierces the disciple's earlobe with a double-edged knife and inserts an iron ring.

While excess and extreme practices characterize some groups of Śaivites, the majority of Śiva worshippers have much in common with Viṣṇu *bhaktas* (devotees). They, too, have their singer saints, whose lyrics are recited at worship. They praise Śiva as Lord and Saviour, and they implore him to help in need, expressing their strong desire to receive his grace. Unlike Vaiśṇavas, Śaivas have a certain history of religious persecution and forced conversion. They probably believed that they owed this use of force to their Lord, whose violence and outbreaks of temper became proverbial in the religious lore of India. However, the same tradition asserts that Śiva is not only quick to get enraged but also quickly appeased and ready to give his blessing to everyone, regardless.

Śiva in art

Some of the most magnificent temple architecture and some of the most outstanding sculptures have been inspired by Śaivism. While most of Northern India's older Śiva temples were destroyed by the Muslim rulers, in South India Hinduism continued more or less undisturbed. Major temple-cities like Cidambaram, Madurai or Mylapore survived and have become major tourist attractions.

Typical of Śaivite temples is an austere interior, in which, usually, only the bare *liṅga* is present as the single sign of Śiva's presence. The outside walls and adjacent halls are usually richly decorated with sculptures representing episodes from the Śaivite scriptures, or portraying Śaivite saints. Frequently one finds images of *Śiva parivāra*, Śiva's family, comprising, besides Śiva, his consort, Umā or Pārvatī, and their sons Skandha and the elephant-headed Gaṇeśa, one of the most popular deities of Hinduism.

Gaṇeśa, who according to tradition was Vyāsa's secretary, wrote down the entire *Mahābhārata* and all the *Purāṇas* as they were dictated to him by Vyāsa. No wonder that he has become the patron deity of all those who write: accountants and authors, journalists and, especially, students. They bring the tools of their trade – books, ledgers, copy-books, probably by this time computers and calculators too – before Gaṇeśa images to secure his blessing.

The story of how Gaṇeśa acquired his elephant head is worth telling. Śiva, in one of his fits of rage, invaded a large gathering and indiscriminately cut off heads and limbs. When his distraught wife complained that he had also decapitated his own son, he quickly repented and promised to restore the boy to life. The head lying next to the corpse happened to be an elephant's; it was tacked onto Gaṇeśa's body, and he has looked like that ever since.

The best known and most important artistic representation of Śiva is that of *Naṭarāja*, Śiva as the Lord of Dance. It encapsulates the entire philosophy of Śaivism. Framed in a circle of flames, the centre is occupied by four-armed Śiva, dancing on a prostrate figure. The dancing Śiva is creator, maintainer and destroyer of the world, as well the one who saves from it. The figure on which his left foot rests is called *āpasmāra*, 'the man of sin', whom he subdues. His right foot is lifted up – it symbolizes Śiva's readiness to absorb his devotee's karma and give his grace. In one hand he carries a drum, symbolizing the sound that saves. In another he carries the fire that destroys the world. In his matted hair nestle snakes, and around his neck he wears a string of skulls, each one representing a Brahmā, the lord of an aeon. Śiva survives them all. The circle of flames symbolizes *saṁsāra*, the fleeting, phenomenal world.

Another image, that of Śiva *Nīlakaṇṭha*, 'Śiva with the dark-blue throat', is often seen. When the gods and demons churned the primaeval milk ocean to obtain *amṛta*, the nectar of immortality, the first product turned out be *halāhalā*, a fiery poison that threatened to consume everything. Śiva, being of a compassionate nature, took it in his hand and swallowed it. It was so powerful that it darkened Śiva's throat – but his action saved the world. Thus for Śaivites Śiva Nīlakaṇṭha has come to symbolize God's salvific intervention and his willingness to sacrifice himself in order to save the world.

While for a long time Western scholars seemed to avoid Śiva and Śaivism, in recent years there has been a great upsurge of interest. Some, like Alain Daniélou and Stella Kramrisch, became initiated into Śaivite orders. Others, like Wendy Doniger, focused a major part of their textual studies on the ambivalent figure of Śiva, who seems so diametrically different from traditional Western notions of God. Intrigued by the fascinating and elusive mythology surrounding Śiva and attracted by the wonderful artistic representations of this god, many have overcome the cultural barriers which former generations had erected. There is a quite active Śaiva Siddhānta mission in the West, too. An American convert, who adopted the name Śivaya Subramuniyaswami, produced a number of books in which Śaivism is explained and adapted to modern Western circumstances.

Suggested further reading

Doniger O'Flaherty, Wendy. *Asceticism and Eroticism in the Mythology of Shiva*. Oxford University Press: London, 1973.

Kramrisch, Stella. *The Presence of Shiva*. Princeton University Press: Princeton, 1981.

Lorenzen, David N. *The Kapalikas and Kalamukhas. Two Lost Shaivite Sects*. University of California Press: Berkeley, 1972.

Sivaraman, Krishna. *Shaivism in Philosophical Perspective*. Motilal Banarsidass: Delhi, 1973.

Siva sanctuary beneath pipal tree

8
The Goddess and her worshippers

India has always retained a tradition of the highest being as Goddess, a notion that was apparently universal in prehistoric times, before patriarchal societies elevated a male God to the highest position of authority. While patriarchy certainly is characteristic of vedic religion – we find the macho Indra at the apex of the vedic pantheon – Goddess worship remained part of that tradition. Some of the most celebrated Goddess hymns, such as the *Vāksūkta* (hymn to Speech), are found in the *Ṛgveda* itself.

Goddess worship has also always been an integral component of Vaiṣṇavism and Śaivism. Viṣṇu without Śri, Rāma without Sītā, Kṛṣṇa without Rādhā are unthinkable. Śaivism has created the interesting figure of Śiva *ardhānarī*, Śiva half woman, half man. According to a popular legend, once upon a time a famous and ardent Śiva worshipper refused to worship Pārvatī, Śiva's consort. Instead of circumambulating both divinities, he slipped through between the two, honouring only Śiva. Śiva, to teach him a lesson, became one person with Pārvatī, so that the devotee could not help worshipping her as he worshipped Śiva. *Śiva ardhānarī* is represented in sculptures in which the right half has all the male, and the left half all the female characteristics of a deity. Śiva tantrikas go so far as to identify the Goddess with the energy (*śakti*) that gives him life: Śiva without *śakti*, identified with the vowel *i*, is *śava*, a lifeless corpse. In addition, Hinduism has also developed Śāktism, a tradition in which the Goddess is the one supreme principle.

Goddess myths and celebrations

The greatest festival of Bengal, where Goddess religion dominates, is *Durgāpūjā*. It extends over nine days and marks a holiday season dedicated to the worship of Devī, whose images are to be found in public places well as temples: in offices and factories, in homes and schools. The image of *Devī Mahiṣāsura Mārdiṇi* represents the sixteen-armed Goddess about to decapitate a buffalo, from whose severed neck emerges the demon figure of *Mahiṣāsura*.

Part of the ceremonies during the nine-day festival is the recitation of the *Devīmāhātmya*, a section of the *Mārkaṇḍeya Purāṇa*, which describes a centuries-long battle between gods and demons that could only be decided by the intervention of the goddess. After the initial defeat of the gods, when *Mahiṣāsura* had become ruler of the world, the *devas* approached Viṣṇu and Śiva, the greatest among them, for help. They admitted their impotence. Out of their combined anger was created Supreme Power, Śakti, the Goddess who took up battle with Mahiṣāsura. Endowed with the weapons of every one of the gods, she killed thousands of demons and their generals. Mahiṣāsura, however, appeared invincible. In his buffalo form he created havoc among Devī's armies. When she was about to catch him with a lasso, he changed into a lion. When she tried to cut him down with her sword he appeared as a human being. When Devī attacked him with bow and arrows, he changed into the shape of an elephant. About to be crushed by Devī's mace, he switched back into his original buffalo form.

The final battle between Devī and Mahiṣāsura is described in a very dramatic way. The Goddess appears in her most frightful form, with eyes bulging and reddened by a powerful potion and red tongue hanging out of her mouth. Eventually she cuts off the demon's head with her sword, thus restoring the gods to their realms and making the earth safe again for humans. The *Devīmāhātmya* concludes with a promise given by the Goddess, to appear again and again, whenever the world is oppressed by demons too powerful to be handled by either Viṣṇu or Śiva. This revelation of her power reassures her worshippers that she will release them from all danger, and finally bring about their emancipation.

Besides the *Devīmāhātmya*, a relatively short text, there are entire *Purāṇas* that give full expositions of the Goddess religion. The *Devī Purāṇa*, also called *Devī Bhāgavata*, is a parallel to the other *Purāṇas*: it narrates how the universe was created by Devī, and relates a great number of Devī myths, containing numerous promises for those who worship the Goddess. It also mentions a very large number of different names of the Goddess and identifies them with forms of Devī worshipped in different parts of the country.

More, perhaps, than in Vaiṣṇavism or Śaivism, local traditions are important in Śaktism. One particular myth explains why: the Goddess, known as Satī, who had married Śiva against her father Dakṣa's will, attended uninvited one of Dakṣa's solemn vedic sacrifices. Dakṣa not only refused to invite Śiva, he publicly insulted him. Satī, deeply hurt, gave up her life. After wrecking Dakṣa's sacrifice thoroughly, Śiva took away Śati's body and cut it up into fifty-one parts. Wherever he dropped one, a *Śāktapīṭha*, a particularly powerful sanctuary of Devī, became established, named after the particular part of her body that was found there. These *Śāktapīṭhas* are still the centres of Goddess worship, found all over India.

Goddess worship becomes very intense in times of epidemics, which are understood as signs of her wrath for having been neglected. Even today at such times, buffaloes, goats and pigeons are sacrificed to the Goddess in order to appease her.

Newspapers from time to time carry reports about human sacrifices or self-immolations to Devī, which in former times were quite frequent and part of the routine of certain temples. The *Bhāgavata Purāṇa* contains the detailed description of a human sacrifice in honour of the Goddess, performed by a chieftain who wanted to have children. Similarly, the *Kālikā Purāṇa*, in its

PRAISING THE GODDESS

Praise be to the Divine Mother,
The inscrutable Power in all things.
Praise be to the Divine Mother,
The Intelligence in all things.
Praise be to the Divine Mother,
The Forgiveness in all things.
Praise be to the Divine Mother,
The Peacefulness in all things.
Praise be to the Divine Mother,
The Faithfulness in all things.
Praise be to the Divine Mother,
The Beauty in all things.
Praise be to the Divine Mother,
The Mercy in all things.
Praise be to the Divine Mother,
The Consciousness in all things.
O Mother, you take away all the sufferings of your devotees,
You are the Mother of the universe,
Let your mercy shine on all.

From the *Devīmāhātmya*

'blood-chapter', offers extensive information on the various bloody sacrifices 'through which the Goddess is pleased'. While by the sacrifice of animals such as buffaloes, goats, rhinoceroses, etc., the Goddess is appeased for a short time, by a human sacrifice, 'properly performed, the Goddess is pleased for a thousand years'.

There is historic evidence that up to the nineteenth century a human sacrifice was performed every Friday in the Kālī temple at Tanjore, in South India. The head of the victim was placed on a golden plate before the image of the Goddess, while the royal family ate rice cooked in its blood, to gain power and strength. Regular human sacrifice to the Goddess was practised for centuries in the Kālī temple in Kāmākhyā, Assam. References to human sacrifices performed by historic personalities (in honour of Devī) are quite frequent, and there is no reason to doubt their truth. In the nineteenth century the British administration waged a decades-long battle against the Thags, a band of murderous thieves, who strangled their victims in order to honour the Goddess, their patron deity.

The idol of the Goddess in the famous Kālī temple in Calcutta, where even now many goats are decapitated every day in honour of Kālī, shows a threatening black figure with a long, red, protruding tongue: the standard representation of Kālī, the fierce goddess, who has been associated with death and bloody sacrifice since time immemorial.

Tantras and yantras

The *Tantras* are a large class of writings of a fairly technical nature: they teach how to attain ultimate freedom and bliss through worship of the Goddess. In them Devī occupies the supreme place. According to them, *brahman*, being neuter and incapable of procreating, produced Śiva and Śakti. Śiva is the cause of bondage, Śakti the force for liberation. She is the life energy of the universe. She is the focus of *tāntrika* practices.

Tantricism is surrounded by an aura of secrecy and mystery. One reason for this is that the so-called 'left-hand *tantra*' involves rituals that violate normal morality and Hindu tradition. The followers of this kind of *tantra* are obliged to keep their membership and ceremonies secret from the rest of the people. This has not hindered some of them from divulging particulars, and today anybody can get hold of the texts and read about the rituals in a number of publications.

'Right-hand *tantra*' in many ways resembles the kind of worship practised by Viṣṇu and Śiva devotees. What is special is the emphasis on *dīkṣā*, initiation, and the use of monosyllabic *bīja-mantras*, 'seed-spells', whose meaning is revealed only to the initiate. An exclusive initiation ceremony, preferably administered by a female *guru*, is the only way to become a *tāntrika*. Membership is open to all without restriction of caste or sex, but even a brahmin has to apply for it, if he wishes to join.

Tantricism regards itself as a kind of spiritual homoeopathy: as a snakebite is cured by a dose of snake poison, so the evil propensities of the human heart are supposed to be cured by a dose of indulgence. The dose must be administered by an expert physician, otherwise great harm would result. The preparation involves the practice of secret *mantras*, syllables like *'hrim'*, *'klim'*, etc., that have no recognizable meaning, except for the initiates, who identify them with aspects of the Goddess.

A major feature of tantricism is the use of *yantras*, geometric patterns of overlapping triangles, circles and squares, which are seen as symbolic representations of the Goddess. Inscribed on the *yantra* are the monosyllabic *mantras*, which together constitute the 'word-body' of the Goddess. The centre is occupied by the word *śri* and the *bindu*, a dot, which symbolizes the very essence of the deity. The whole pattern is designed to lead worshippers into an extended meditation on all aspects of the deity, and to make them realize the Goddess as the inmost core of themselves and of all things.

Tantricism identifies Śakti with *prakṛti* (nature, matter), rather than with spirit. The body, then, becomes the seat of the divinity. The fifty letters of the Sanskrit alphabet constitute the body of the Goddess as well as that of the worshipper. Through the ritual called *nyāsa*, 'depositing', the worshipper transfers the letters from the *yantra* to different parts of his body, thus transforming it, limb by limb, into a divine entity.

In many forms of *tāntrika* worship the awakening of *Kuṇḍalinī śakti* plays a role: the secret divine power is believed to lie dormant in the body, coiled up like a snake around the base of the spine. Through *Tantrayoga* it is believed to be awakened and sent through six centres, called *cakras*, along the spinal cord, till it meets with Śiva, seated in the thousand-petalled lotus in the top of the head. *Tāntrikas* have developed an elaborate physiology of the 'subtle body', which is formed by thirty-five million *nāḍis* (fine tubes), through which Śakti moves. Three of these, called Iḍā, Piṇgalā and Suṣumnā, form the central complex. The individual parts of the subtle body are identified with various deities, virtues and accomplishments, and the adept believes that through the process of Kuṇḍalinī yoga he absorbs all these into his own being, thus becoming 'everything'.

The renewal of Goddess worship

The age-old and often esoteric traditions of Śāktism have met with renewed interest in recent times in feminist circles. Here we have a religion that gives not only equality, but also superiority to the female principle, and provides a rich symbolism of women-power. Some of that symbolism has even been transferred to Western religions, and it is no longer unheard of to refer to God as Mother rather than Father.

In India, too, there is a renewal and re-interpretation of Goddess traditions in the wake of modern developments. Śāktism, in one form or other, has become an element of virtually all branches of Hinduism. It has become more emphasized in recent decades due to the influence of major figures such as Rāmakrishna Paramahamsa and Aurobindo Ghose.

Rāmakrishna (1834–86), whose name is linked with a world-wide organization, the Ramakrishna Mission, became famous in his lifetime as the ecstatic priest of the Kālī temple in Dakshineshwar, near Calcutta. He spent hours in trance before the image of the Goddess, and in his discourses he delved into the mysteries of Devī's being and working. Nevertheless, he encouraged a broad understanding of religion, considering all traditions as essentially one.

Similarly, Aurobindo Ghose (1872–1950), one of the most influential Indian thinkers of the twentieth century, reconceived Śāktism in the light of contemporary philosophy and science. His 'Integral Yoga' is strongly influenced by the Kuṇḍalinī tradition, but it also goes far beyond it.

To many contemporary Hindus the Goddess today appears as 'Mother Earth' and ecological efforts are seen as expressions of service and worship to Devī. Thus symbolic acts of traditional Goddess worship and concrete actions to prevent pollution of a river, preserve a forest, or save an area from flooding by hydro-electric projects become integral parts of a new expression of Śāktism.

V. S. Agrawala called 'Mother Earth' the 'deity of the new age': 'The modern age offers its salutations to Mother Earth whom it adores as the Super-Goddess.' He sees her realized both in the physical landscape of India and in her culture: 'Mother Earth is born of contemplation. Let the people devote themselves truthfully to the Mother Land whose legacy they have received from the ancients.'

The making of new Goddesses

It is fairly typical for Hindus to worship a human person who exhibits special qualities of body or mind as a manifestation of the divine. Frequently people see in dreams visions of recently deceased women who request that a shrine be built in their honour, promising to protect their loved ones. Usually the person who has appeared in this way is identified with an established goddess, such as Mariammā, the smallpox goddess. Such Goddess cults flourish especially in villages, where villagers seek protection from the many threats and dangers to their lives. This belief in the power of the goddesses is so strong that in many places villagers have been known to refuse to submit to mandatory smallpox inoculation because the goddess Mariammā had appeared to some and warned them to kill those who had more faith in newfangled science than in her own power to heal.

Analogously, women with great political power such as Indira Gandhi, or spiritual fame, such as Anandamayi, were considered by many to be incarnations of the Goddess. This folk belief connects with a Hindu tradition requiring that newly anointed kings sought the authorization of the local Goddess temple before they could exercise their power. The seal of authority which the king gave to his officers, the *mudrā*, was an expression of *śakti*, the power of the Goddess.

While Hinduism for centuries extolled the eternal spirit over the transient body, and devised ascetic strategies designed to suppress desire, Śāktism deifies the life-force and worships the bodily expressions of the Goddess. This makes it attractive to an age that has little use for self-denial and does not recognize a spirit-reality over and above the world of ordinary experience. Goddess worship leads back to the origins and to a state of mind where the undivided consciousness reigns supreme.

Suggested further reading

Bharati, Agehananda. *The Tantric Tradition*. Rider & Co.: London, 1965.

Brown, C. M. *God as Mother: A Feminine Theology in India*. Claude Stark: Connecticut, 1974.

Kinsley, David R. *The Sword and the Flute: Dark Visions of the Terrible and the Sublime in Hindu Mythology*. University of California Press: Berkeley, 1975.

—— *Hindu Goddesses*. University of California Press: Berkeley, 1986.

Part III
The Hindu Philosophical Quest

Since ancient times India had been famous for its wisdom and its thought. The ancient Persians, Greeks and Romans were eager to learn from its sages and philosophers. The brahmins had a wide reputation for leading saintly lives and engaging in a deep philosophical quest. When Alexander the Great invaded north-west India in 324 BCE, one of his greatest desires was to meet Indian philosophers. One of them, whom the Greeks called Kalanos, became his permanent adviser. A fictitious but certainly ancient exchange of letters between Alexander and an Indian king praises the purity of life and the deep wisdom of the brahmins. Further, Pythagoras is said to have learned the principles of his philosophy and lifestyle – he believed in the transmigration of the soul and insisted on a vegetarian diet – from Indian sources. The parallels between Platonism and Vedānta are striking, and the Neoplatonist Apollonius of Tyana spent years in India before setting out to teach. Even the great Plotinus, after learning from the best authorities in Egypt, joined a military expedition of Emperor Gordian in order to gain firsthand knowledge of Indian philosophy.

Throughout the Middle Ages, when there was no direct contact between Europe and India, the great reputation of Indian wisdom remained proverbial. When, in the eighteenth century, the first translations of some *Upaniṣads* and the *Bhagavadgītā* became available to the West, European philosophers rhapsodized about the profundity and beauty of these writings. Here they encountered a fusion of philosophy and religion, a deep wisdom and a concern with the ultimate, that had no parallel in either contemporary Western philosophy or Western religion. While much of the first enthusiasm may have been founded on very superficial knowledge and inadequate translations, further scholarly research certainly confirmed the reputation of Indian thought.

It is a fact that in India philosophy and theology were never divorced, as happened in the West from the sixteenth century onwards. Philosophical reflection is an integral part of an educated Hindu's understanding of religion. An introduction to Hinduism, however short and elementary, cannot be adequate without at least a brief introduction to Indian philosophy. Much of this is highly sophisticated and very technical. It surpasses, both in volume and in subtlety, much of Western philosophy and requires intensive and extensive study. But some of its principles and some of its applications to religious issues should be understandable also to non-specialists.

In contrast to former times, when one had to rely on few and often inadequate translations of sources and little help was offered by scholarly writings, today an immense amount of well-translated source-material and scholarly studies of many aspects of Indian philosophy are available. However sketchy the following chapters are, and however esoteric some might sound, they may induce some readers to make a deeper study, which they will certainly find most rewarding.

THE PHILOSOPHICAL SCHOOLS OF HINDUISM

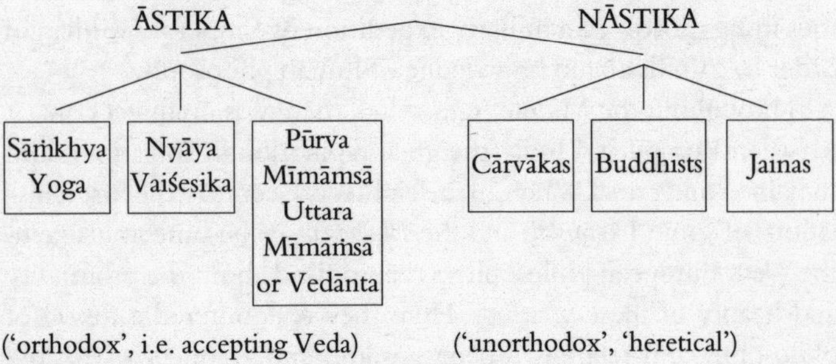

('orthodox', i.e. accepting Veda) [Ṣaḍdarśanas] ('unorthodox', 'heretical')

9
The wisdom of the Upaniṣads

The *Upaniṣads*, also called *Vedānta*, 'End of the Veda', have been for thousands of years the main inspiration of Hindu religious philosophy. Though originally composed by and for people who had reached the last stage of their lives and no longer shared the cares and hopes of those who were actively engaged in social life and ritualistic religion, the *Upaniṣads* serve as a kind of 'primary philosophy', a fundamental metaphysics for all of philosophically inclined Hinduism. Their language and their insights are also part of the popular *Purāṇas* and *Tantras*, as well as of hymns and prayers used in daily worship. Accepted as *śruti*, as part of vedic revelation, the *Upaniṣads* are not only seen as conveying human wisdom but as providing liberating truth. Some of their utterances, the so-called *mahāvākyas*, 'Great Sayings', are considered as verbal expressions of ultimate freedom itself.

The *Upaniṣads* are not modern-style philosophy text-books. They offer their teaching in a largely unsystematic, aphoristic manner, using parables, stories, metaphors. As a class of writings they do not express one unified philosophy, but juxtapose parallel views. The thirty-two *vidyās*, 'paths to knowledge', identified by scholars as distinct teachings in the *Upaniṣads*, all convey methods for reaching ultimate freedom. The underlying theories of reality and the methods suggested for finding enlightenment, however, are enormously varied.

The four stages of knowledge

The *Upaniṣads* leave no doubt that the knowledge they teach is hard to obtain and requires long and strenuous effort. A story contained in the *Chāndogya Upaniṣad* illustrates this: Prajāpati announces that the knowledge of the true self would bring fulfilment of all desires, freedom from death and sickness, liberation from all evils. Indra, the leader of the gods, and the demon king Virocana, both hear that message and decide to seek that knowledge from Prajāpati. After accepting them as students, Prajāpati lets them work for him for thirty-two years without telling them anything more about the true Self. He eventually asks them the purpose of their coming. When they state it in his very own words, he tells them to put on their best clothes, adorn themselves, and then look into a mirror. They do so, and apparently like what they see. They leave under the impression that they have found ultimate insight into the nature of the self.

Virocana, the demon king, announces to his subjects that bodily enjoyment and happiness is the ultimate wisdom of the Self, but Indra, the king of the gods, has second thoughts: the body whose image he beheld can undergo all kinds of afflictions. A person might become blind, lame, crippled – a self identical with the body will suffer and perish with it. Indra then goes back to Prajāpati to learn more about the immortal Self.

Another thirty-two years of waiting and working pass before Prajāpati reveals a further insight: the true and immortal Self is the one that moves about freely in dreams, unhindered by bodily restrictions. After initially rejoicing at this revelation Indra again begins to reflect: not all dreams are happy dreams; sometimes one experiences fright and anguish. A self identical with the dreamer cannot be called unconditionally happy. He then returns to Prajāpati, who commends his sagacity and promises to teach him about the true immortal Self after another period of thirty-two years.

Next Prajāpati tells him: he who dwells in deep, dreamless sleep is the immortal and blissful Self. Again Indra, for a short period satisfied with the answer, returns to Prajāpati, explaining his doubts: one who sleeps may be happy, but he does not know it. After waking up he has no recollection of his happiness. Prajāpati asks him to stay for five more years to learn the ultimate secret: everything connected with the body is ephemeral, unsatisfactory, painful. Only one who is free of the body is free from fear, pain, ageing and death. The true Self is that bodiless spirit dwelling in us that must emancipate itself from all bodily bonds: only then can immortality and eternal bliss be found.

Two lessons can be gleaned from this story. The first is that if it takes the King of the Gods a full century to understand the true nature of the Self, ordinary mortals should not expect it to come easily. A lifetime, even several lifetimes, may be required. The second lesson is the teaching of the four stages of consciousness and knowledge that is basic to Upaniṣadic instruction. As Indra is led successively to understand the differences in self-perception in waking, dreaming and dreamless sleep, so every student of Vedānta has to learn that, corresponding to the various states of consciousness, there are different perceptions of reality. It is telling that for the *Upaniṣads* the 'normal' waking state (*jāgrita*), in which sense-perception and rational thought shape perceptions of reality, is considered the lowest. In that condition the self is fragmented and identifies with a myriad objects, and is subject to time and space and the laws that govern the physical world. Over against this, dreaming (*svapna*) is considered to provide a higher perception: the dreaming self is no longer tied to the laws of logic or the constraints of space and time. Dreamless sleep (*suṣupti*) constitutes a condition in which all the faculties of the self are unified, and which is remembered as blissful. The highest condition, however, is the 'Fourth State' (*turīya*), which can no longer be described in terms of empirical reality. It is pure awareness, consciousness of consciousness, complete emancipation from all limitations which the body imposed on the self. The 'Fourth State' is the true nature of the Self – immortal, blissful, independent.

The self and the all: *ātman* and *brahman*

Self-knowledge, not in a psychological but in a metaphysical sense, is the only real concern of the *Upaniṣads*: to know the Self means to be the Self, to have found one's destiny. The *Upaniṣads* go one step further: they claim that by knowing the Self one knows everything, by being the Self one becomes the Absolute. *Ātman* is *brahman* – this is the profoundest insight they teach. Again, it is through stories and illustrations that we are led to understand this.

The *Bṛhadāraṇyaka Upaniṣad* reports a lively discussion between the legendary sage Yājñavalkya and his wife Gārgī about the structure of the universe, which is assumed to possess a multi-layered texture: the world, Gārgī has learned, is 'woven, warp and woof, on water'. On what is water woven? On wind, says Yājñavalkya. And wind? On sky. And so on. The entire ancient cosmology is played through. Finally, Yājñavalkya explains that the 'world of the Lord of Creation' is woven on *brahman*. Gārgī continues the questioning: 'And on what is the world of *brahman* woven, warp and woof?' Yājñavalkya cautions: 'Gārgī, you are asking too much about the Divine Being, about which we are not supposed to question too much. Gārgī, do not question too much!'

There is nothing beyond *brahman* – it is the end of all being and of all questioning. But only someone who has reached the highest state of consciousness can know that. The knowledge of the ultimate is not an infinite sum of detailed knowledge about the world, but the transcending of it. One arrives at it not by scientifically investigating the universe but by leaving behind as unsatisfactory all knowledge based on sense-perception and inference. The famous Upaniṣadic formula *neti, neti* ('not this, not so') expresses it best: every attempt to identify the ultimate with something must be rejected as insufficient. The ultimate ground of all is no-thing; *brahman* defies definition in terms other than itself.

Another episode from the *Chāndogya Upaniṣad* will illustrate this. Uddālaka welcomes his son Śvetaketu back from his twelve years' sojourn with his teacher. He has mastered all the subjects of traditional vedic learning and is quite proud of it. His father enquires about his studies: 'Did you also ask for that teaching whereby what has not been heard of becomes heard of, what has not been thought of, becomes thought of, what has not been understood, becomes understood?' Śvetaketu has to confess his ignorance on these matters and suspects that his own teacher did not know them. Thus Uddālaka offers to teach Śvetaketu about that One, by knowing whom everything is known. He does so through some practical experiments.

He first asks Śvetaketu to bring a fig. Śvetaketu does so. 'Open it up. What do you see?' 'There are tiny seeds in it.' 'Divide one of the seeds. What do you see?' 'Nothing' is the answer. But Uddālaka tells him: 'The subtle substance which you cannot perceive, that is the source of this mighty tree. That which appears so tiny is the *ātman* of all. This is the true Self, that *you* are, Śvetaketu!'

Another experiment follows: Śvetaketu is asked to bring a vessel filled with water and to taste it. He is also asked to bring some salt and taste it. He then has to throw a handful of salt into the water and taste it again. Whereas at first all the water had tasted sweet, now all the water tastes salty. The salt has become one with the water, inseparable, but it clearly is a different substance, as Śvetaketu knows. And the father concludes: 'That which is the most subtle substance, that is the *ātman* of the whole world. That is Reality. That *you* are (*tat tvam asi*).'

The profoundest truth which the *Upaniṣads* have to teach is this: there is a ground of being that permeates all and structures all; the visible world is but a transformation, a modification of part of it.

While the phenomena are transient, the ground of being itself is eternal, unchanging. This ground of being can be realized by humans in their innermost consciousness. At the most intimate level *ātman* and *brahman* are identical: *tat tvam asi*,'that', the ultimate being, *you* are.

It is only at the level of the 'Fourth State' of consciousness that this identity is attained and understood; it would be a dangerous mistake to equate the self as perceived in the normal waking state with the ultimate. For someone who, through a long process of interiorization, has reached the state of *turīya*, the Fourth State, the insight into the identity of reality, is self-evident. To reach that state a long process of physical and spiritual discipline is required, a continuous *neti, neti*, a total rejection of all other solutions to one's problems.

THE NATURE OF BRAHMAN

This is the truth:

As sparks fly from a large fire by the thousands,
So from the Imperishable manifold beings are produced
Only to return.

The Great One is without form, like ether,
Within and without, unborn, breathless, mindless, pure,
It is higher than the Imperishable.

The Great One brings forth breath, mind, and all the senses,
Space, wind, light, water, and earth, who supports all.
Its head is fire, its eyes sun and moon, its ears space.
Its voice are the Vedas, its breath the wind,
Its heart is the whole world.

Truly, this is the Inner Self of all.

Muṇḍaka Upaniṣad, II.I.1–5

Liberation from rebirth: *mokṣa*

Since the time of the *Upaniṣads* belief in rebirth has been intimately associated with Hinduism. Rebirth (*punar-janma*) is regarded as fact by Hindus, and efforts to bring the endless cycle of births and deaths to an end are at the core of all Hindu religious practices. The prospect of having to die, time and again, all kinds of deaths (*punar-mṛtyu*), of having to endure existences not only as lowly humans, but as animals and plants, is so frightening that everything must be done to avoid it. There is no natural evolution that automatically brings an end to rebirth. Only the great discoveries of the Upaniṣadic sages made it possible to achieve liberation from rebirth and repeated death.

For Hindus, the very fact of our existence in these particular bodies proves the existence of *karma* and the law of rebirth. Why else would we be different from each other, why else would we be on earth? We come into the world at birth with a load of *karma* produced by our actions in previous lives. This *prārabdha karma* is augmented by the *karma* acquired in the course of our present life. Hindus believe that actions inexorably produce effects: good deeds result in good *karma*, which produces good fortune; evil deeds result in bad *karma*, which sooner or later results in punishment. To leave the cycle of births and deaths, the chain that binds actions, rewards and punishments to *karma* has to be cut through.

The solution which was offered by the *Bhagavadgītā* was that *niṣkāma karma* (desireless action) focused on God does not result in binding *karma*, but leads to release. The *Upaniṣads* offer a different path: *jñāna* (insight, wisdom, knowledge) saves from *karma* and rebirth. Since the realization of *turīya*, the Fourth State, occurs at a level beyond bodily perception, it no longer creates *karma*, which is inexorably tied to the body and its activities. When all consciousness is withdrawn from the senses and the mind and focused on the ultimate, all awareness of bodily functions and conditions ceases. The person who has reached that state no longer speaks of the body as 'I' or of conditions affecting a body that is 'mine'. In that sense the *Upaniṣads* can truthfully speak of liberation from sickness, old age and death. This *mokṣa* (release) consists not only in annihilation of bodily consciousness, but in expansion of consciousness to everything: *ātman* is *brahman*.

The chief means of reaching this point is the practice of *viveka*, 'discrimination', between the Self and the Not-Self. Whatever is transient, whatever has come into existence and goes out of existence, whatever belongs to the world of *dvandvas* (polar opposites), belongs to the sphere of the Not-Self and must be left behind. The Self is beginningless and deathless, it is by its own nature pure and sinless. Liberation, then, is not 'going somewhere' or 'leaving the world', but the realization of a condition which always existed, but was unrecognized. This is the reason why the role of *vidyā* (knowledge, wisdom) is so much emphasized.

Vidyā is not knowledge of things outside ourselves, but knowledge of our true condition, of our being eternal and free. The *Chāndogya Upaniṣad* explains: 'As water does not cling to a lotus leaf, so *karma* does not cling to one who knows *brahman*.' The oneness of knowing and being, imperfectly seen in the realm of knowledge which is based on sense experience, fully applies at the highest state: 'One who knows *brahman* becomes *brahman*.'

The attainment of the highest condition does not imply a transformation of mortal into immortal, material into spiritual, but a radical separation of the *ātman* from everything else. Indian philosophical anthropology does not dichotomize the human body into body and soul but identifies three components:

- the gross, material body (*sthūla śarīra*)
- the subtle, 'karmic' body (*sūkṣma śarīra*)
- the *ātman*.

Most of the faculties which in Western tradition are associated with the soul, such as rational thought, feeling, memory, etc., are in Indian terminology attributed to the subtle body. It makes no sense, then, to translate *ātman* as 'soul'; we would do better to leave it untranslated. The only statement that can be made about *ātman* is that it is consciousness. It is wholly unrelated to the body. If and when a person reaches *mokṣa*, both the subtle and the gross body become unrelated to the *ātman*.

One of the questions debated in later vedantic philosophy is the possibility of a *jīvanmukti*, liberation while still in a physical body. While some schools categorically deny such a possibility, others affirm it. They think that it is possible to live the life of emancipation while still in a body. Untouched and untroubled by physical and psychic phenomena, such a 'liberated-in-life' person (*jīvanmukta*) would serenely wait for death – a death that does not bring about any change in consciousness.

The great sayings

Four particular, short sentences in the *Upaniṣads* have been singled out as *mahāvākyas*, 'Great Sayings'. They embody, especially in the opinion of the Advaitins, the essence of Upaniṣadic wisdom, and are supposed to have inherent power to bring about the realization of the identity of *ātman* and *brahman*. They are also used as initiation *mantras* by members of the Daśanāmi *saṁnyāsis*, the orders of ascetics organized by Śaṅkara in the ninth century. One of them has already been mentioned: *tat tvam asi*, 'that you are' (*Chāndogya Upaniṣad* VI, 8, 7). Another is *aham brahmāsmi*, 'I am *brahman*' (*Bṛhadāraṇyaka Upaniṣad* I, 4). The other two are *ayam ātma brahma*: 'This Self is the Ultimate' (*Bṛhadāraṇyaka Upaniṣad* II, 5,19), and *prajñānam brahma*: '*brahman* is wisdom' (*Aitareya Upaniṣad* III, 1,13). The adept is to meditate on these profound statements until their content becomes no longer a teaching imparted by someone from the outside, but one's own experience. Their truth is obvious only at the level of *turīya*, the Fourth State. To apply them to lower states of consciousness would be patently false and inappropriate.

THE TEN PRINCIPAL SCHOOLS OF VEDĀNTA, THEIR FOUNDERS AND THEIR MAIN WORK (COMMENTARY ON *BRAHMASŪTRA*)

1. ADVAITA VEDĀNTA – Śaṅkara (788–820 CE): *Śarīrakabhāṣya*
2. VIŚIṢṬĀDVAITA VEDĀNTA – Rāmānuja (1017–1137 CE): *Śrībhāṣya*
3. DVAITA VEDĀNTA – Madhva (1238–1317 CE): *Aṇuvakhyāyana*
4. BHEDĀBHEDA – Bhāskara (9th century): *Brahmasūtrabhāṣya*
5. DVAITĀDVAITA: Nimbārka (llth century): *Vedāntaparijātasaurabha*
6. ŚUDDHĀDVAITA – Vallabha (1473–1531 CE): *Aṇubhāṣya*
7. ACINTYA BHEDĀBHEDA: Baladeva (18th century): *Govindabhāṣya*
8. DVAITĀDVAITA: Śrīpati (1350–1410 CE): *Śrīkārabhāṣya*
9. ŚIVĀDVAITA – Śrīkaṇṭha (13th century): *Śrīkaṇṭhabhāṣya*
10. SĀMĀNYAVĀDA – Vijñānabhīkṣu (16th century): *Vijñānāmṛta*

In one way or other the basic ideas of the *Upaniṣads* have become appropriated by all major schools of Hinduism. Interpretations of the words of the *Upaniṣads*, however, vary widely. For some, like Śaṅkara and his school of Advaita Vedānta, the *Upaniṣads* teach absolute monism: there is only one reality, *brahman/ātman*, and it is identical with our depth-consciousness. Others, like Rāmānuja with his Śrīvaiṣṇavas, say that the *Upaniṣads* teach a qualified monism: while the ultimate reality is all-encompassing and omnipresent, the difference between the Supreme Person and individual persons is real, and remains so, even after liberation. Obviously there is no one way to read the *Upaniṣads* – a fact which has given rise to a proliferation of Indian systems of philosophy inspired by them. A modern Western student of the *Upaniṣads* will both be puzzled and amazed by them: the total picture may remain unclear, but there are gems of wisdom and pearls of insight that provide guidance in our quest for our true identity.

Suggested further reading

Doniger O'Flaherty, Wendy (ed.). *Karma and Rebirth in Classical Indian Traditions*. University of California Press: Berkeley, 1980.

Neufeldt, Ron (ed.). *Karma and Rebirth: Post-classical Developments*. State University of New York Press: Albany, NY, 1986.

Radhakrishnan, Sarvepalli. *The Principal Upanishads*. Allen & Unwin: London, 1953.

Ranade, R. D. *A Constructive Survey of Upanishadic Philosophy*. Bharatiya Vidya Bhavan: Bombay, 1968.

10 The philosophy of yoga

Probably everyone has heard the word *Yoga* and knows places where it is taught. Its association with India is beyond doubt, and it is certainly central to Hinduism. However, Yoga has many meanings and comes in many forms. It is also based on an underlying philosophy that is linked to other schools of Indian thought. Yoga, derived from the root *yuj* (to yoke, to join, to combine), is frequently used in India as a synonym for 'religious practice', or for a system of philosophy or religion. Vedāntins interpret Yoga as return of the individual *ātman* to the Supreme. The Yoga with which most Westerners are familiar is *Haṭha Yoga*, consisting of bodily exercises. The Philosophy of Yoga, with which we are dealing here, is also called *Rāja Yoga* (the 'royal' path), or *Pātañjala Yoga*, referring to Patañjali, the reputed author of the *Yogasūtras*, the basic Yoga manual. Because of its close connection with the philosophical system of *Sāṁkhya*, it is also known as *Sāṁkhya-Yoga*. This needs a short explanation. Since virtually all of India's systems of philosophy and theology utilize Sāṁkhya terminology, it is important to go into some technical detail.

The Sāṁkhya system

Sāṁkhya, like all other Indian philosophical systems, aims to offer help in gaining freedom from suffering. In order to do so effectively, it has to analyse the nature of the world in which we live and identify the causes of suffering. Sāṁkhya postulates a fundamental dualism of spirit (*puruṣa*) and matter (*prakṛti*), and locates the cause of suffering in a process of evolution that progressively involves spirit in matter. *Prakṛti* is constituted by three principles (*guṇas*) which are in an unstable equilibrium:

- *sattva*, or lightness
- *rajas*, or impetus
- *tamas*, or inertia.

Originally *puruṣa*, which is conceived as male, is the very opposite of *prakṛti*, which is regarded as female: while he possesses consciousness, she is without it. However, their combination and interaction makes *puruṣa* experience the qualities of *prakṛti* as his own; the evolution of the macrocosm and microcosm takes place, producing a hierarchically ordered universe. There is no need of a creator, since everything is predetermined.

The first and most fundamental entity to develop *is mahat* (the Great One), also called *buddhi* (intellect). From *mahat* issues *ahaṁkāra* (egoity, 'mine-ness'), the principle of individuation. Then the senses develop in the person, corresponding to the material elements in the physical universe. The core of the Sāṁkhya system consists of the classification and enumeration of twenty-four *tattvas*, basic principles or elements out of which the whole world is constituted, *puruṣa* being the twenty-fifth. The purpose of this scheme is to provide correct analysis of the genesis of the universe both 'out there' and within, and so provide a map that can be used to retrace the steps to the source.

The imbalance of the three *guṇas* causes all movement and unrest in the world and, according to the preponderance of one of them, one is born into a particular body. If *sattva* predominates, one becomes a *deva* or a saint. A predominance of *rajas* results in birth as an ordinary human being. In animals *tamas* is the dominant quality. Being part of the universe that resulted from the interaction between *puruṣa* and *prakṛti* makes one part of the endless cycle of *saṁsāra*, the ever-changing world, and, consequently, of the suffering that goes with it. The 'threefold misery', i.e. the pains and frustrations caused by superhuman beings, by fellow-humans, and by beasts and inanimate objects, as well as by oneself, make human beings seek for an escape from it. It emerges that, since all misery is the result of involvement with the process of becoming, the end of all misery is to be found in the *puruṣa's* dissociation from *prakṛti*. *Puruṣa* by his very nature is free and cannot be bound, except in combination with *prakṛti*.

The process of the *puruṣa's* liberation from the attractions of *prakṛti* is described in a telling metaphor: *prakṛti* is likened to a dancer performing for *puruṣa*. Her repertoire being limited, after a while she has to repeat her act over and over again. *Puruṣa*, having watched the same scenes time after time, loses interest. *Prakṛti*, realizing that *puruṣa* is no longer paying attention, ceases to dance. Translated into plain language this means that after a person has lived for some time, there is nothing new and exciting about life any longer. A person's desires diminish in proportion to the lack of attractions life offers. One's spirit becomes aware of its peculiar nature as different from the body, and withdraws into itself. For some time, as long as the union of spirit and matter continues in a living body, life goes on, as the *Sāṁkhya Kārikās* say, 'just as the potter's wheel continues to turn without being driven, due to the previously imparted momentum'. When *puruṣa* and *prakṛti* finally separate, all activity ceases: *prakṛti* becomes mere passive potentiality, and *puruṣa* reaches *kaivalya* ('alone-ness'), perfect freedom and spiritual self-satisfaction.

The *Yogasūtras* of Patañjali

Patañjali is one of the great names of the Hindu tradition. His identity, however, cannot be satisfactorily ascertained. Tradition identifies Patañjali, the author of the *Yogasūtras*, with Patañjali, the author of the *Mahābhāṣya*, a text on Sanskrit grammar, and Patañjali, the author of the *Cārakasaṁhitā*, one of the famous books on Indian medicine. Thus Patañjali becomes the universal physician: he offers health and help to body, mind and soul. The *Yogasūtras* are clearly a summary of many earlier works, and some scholars, like Gerhard Oberhammer, think they present an epitome of not one but several different 'yogas'. For present purposes here they are treated as describing one path, although the text digresses quite often and goes back and forth in its treatment of Yoga.

If Sāṁkhya describes the evolution of matter, its diversification into a manifold, Yoga describes the process of reducing multiplicity to Oneness. Making use of the terms coined by Sāṁkhya and taking over its world-picture, the *Yogasūtras* describe the practice of the process of discriminative knowledge that leads to the liberation of the embodied spirit. Yoga is not mere theory, although it is one of the philosophical systems. It also implies physical training, will-power and decisions. It deals with the human condition as a whole and aims at providing real freedom, not just a theory of liberation. Although much of its concern is psychological, it differs radically from contemporary Western psychology: it assumes the reality of a spirit-soul, has a strong ethical orientation, and focuses on states of consciousness that simply are not recognized by the modern West.

The *Yogasūtras* are a short work containing 194 brief aphorisms arranged in four parts entitled:

- *samādhi* (concentration)
- *sādhana* (practice)
- *vibhuti* (extraordinary faculties)
- *kaivalya* (ultimate freedom).

The text itself, however, is less systematic than this division would suggest. The Yoga described in the *Yogasūtras* has also been described as *aṣṭāṅga yoga*, 'eight-limbed Yoga'. While not covering all the aphorisms, this designation provides a convenient and logical scheme to describe Patañjali's Yoga. Before presenting this, a few clarifications of basic assumptions may be helpful.

The second *sūtra* defines Yoga as *citta-vṛtti-nirodha*, 'quieting all fluctuations of the mind'. *Citta* (mind) is identical with the *mahat* (the Great One) or the *buddhi* (the mind) of the Sāṁkhya system. It is the first-evolved, and its fluctuations, vibrations and irritations (*vṛttis*) cause the origin of all thoughts and things. If they cease, the mind is free.

The impulse to seek that condition of freedom is given by the experience of *kleśas* (afflictions) that beset life. They are identified as:

- *avidyā* (ignorance, illusion)
- *āsmitā* ('mine-ness', egoism)
- *rāga* (passion, attraction)
- *dveṣa* (aversion, hatred)
- *abhiniveṣa* (fear of death, attachment to life).

While most of these terms are self-explanatory, it is interesting to learn what the *Yogasūtras* mean by the term *avidyā*. It is explained as 'mistaking the transient, impure and evil non-self for the eternal, pure and blissful Self'. This *avidyā* is both the root cause of our unhappiness, and the reason for our seeking liberation.

The eightfold practice of yoga

Aṣṭāṅga Yoga, the yoga practice consisting of eight steps, can be schematically presented as shown on the following page:

THE EIGHT STEPS OF AṢṬĀṄGA YOGA

A. Remote preparation:

1. *yama* (practice of precepts)
   i) *ahiṁsa* (non-violence)
   ii) *satya* (truthfulness)
   iii) *asteya* (non-stealing)
   iv) *brahmacarya* (continence)
   v) *aparigraha* (absence of greed)

2. *niyama* (practice of virtues)
   i) *śauca* (purity)
   ii) *saṁtoṣa* (contentment)
   iii) *tapas* (discipline)
   iv) *svādhyāya* (study, especially of sacred lore)
   v) *īśvara praṇidhāna* (surrender to God)

3. *āsana* (postures)

4. *prāṇayama* (breath control)

5. *pratyāhāra* (withdrawal of senses)

B. Direct preparation:

6. *dhāraṇa* (concentration)

7. *dhyāna* (contemplation)

8. *samādhi* (trance)

} these three are collectively called *samyama* (effort) and are successively applied to various categories of objects

C. Beginning of real yoga
which comprises the exercise of extraordinary powers, the practice of advanced forms of meditation, leading to *kaivalya*, (complete isolation and freedom)

The practice of precepts and virtues is preliminary to Yoga, but considered indispensable. If a person has no ethical grounding, the powers acquired through the Yoga practices proper could be used for evil purposes. The practice of virtues also produces many side-effects that are helpful either to the practitioners themselves or to fellow-humans. Thus the *Yogasūtras* assert that in the presence of one who is grounded in *ahiṁsā* (non-violence), others will give up their enmity, and even wild animals become tame. The *Yogasūtras* also give practical advice on how to attain these virtues and how to counteract opposite trends. They analyse the root of all evil tendencies as lying in the triad of

- *lobha* (greed)
- *moha* (delusion)
- *krodha* (anger)

and offer suggestions on how to deal with these root vices in order to eradicate all sins.

While the Yoga that is taught in the West usually concentrates on learning a variety of postures that are supposed to be beneficial to health, Pantañjali says that any posture may be assumed that is agreeable and that allows a practitioner to sit in meditation for a length of time. The aim of *Rājayoga* is neither self-mortification nor physical exercise, but the achievement of inner freedom.

In certain circles much is made of the extraordinary faculties which a Yogi is supposed to acquire, such as making oneself as small as an atom or as large as a mountain; understanding the languages of all peoples and even of animals; reading other people's minds; making oneself invisible, etc. Yet the *Yogasūtras* discourage the practitioner from cultivating them, because they are more of a hindrance than a help on the path to freedom. There are certain dietary rules to be observed as well: a Yogi is to avoid spicy food, everything pungent, sour, or salty. Again, while the use of drugs, especially *bhaṅg* (hashish), is widespread among Yogis in India, Patañjali discourages this practice. *Kaivalya* is a state of mind that should be achieved without any involvement of foreign substances.

Reaching *kaivalya*

Breath-control, *prāṇayama*, is a central practice in Yoga. The *Upaniṣads* contain many speculations on *prāṇa* (breath of life), and controlling one's breathing is an ancient and widely practised method of purification. Some Yogis succeed in controlling their breathing to such an extent that they can reduce their metabolism to the point where they can be buried for days or even weeks, and emerge alive. The *Yogasūtras* do not encourage such extraordinary feats, but they consider breath-control basic. Similarly the ability to withdraw one's senses, *pratyāhāra*, is essential. The senses, no longer occupied with transmitting impulses from the body, cease to hinder the mind from functioning according to its own 'mental' mode.

The most crucial exercise, however, is *samyama* (effort), consisting of the triad of *dhāraṇa-dhyāna-samādhi*, 'concentration-contemplation-trance'. They are not seen as flowing from a special psychic capability, but as resulting from strenuous effort. They completely interiorize consciousness, and separate self-consciousness from everything that is not Self, i.e. the body and sense-objects. By applying the technique to a number of dimensions of reality, the Yogi both identifies with and transcends each realm. The detail in which the *Yogasūtras* describe the process is highly technical, and must be studied under the guidance of an experienced teacher. From a certain point in the practice of Yoga, the process becomes irreversible: *kaivalya* (complete introversion) becomes the 'natural' goal of the practitioner's mind. The state of mind shortly before reaching the final stage is defined as *dharma-megha-samādhi* ('*dharma* -cloud trance') in which the finite elementary nature of all things becomes experientially apparent to the Yogi. A kind of zero-time experience precedes the entry into timelessness. *Kaivalya* is described as the spirit 'finding its own true state of nature', the coming home of the soul from the exile of involvement in the process of material evolution.

Yoga, as taught by Patañjali, has a thrust that is diametrically opposed to many of our 'normal' aspirations. It also goes against the flow of mainstream Western philosophies and religions. Nevertheless, it has been found attractive by many of our Western contemporaries. It seems to offer a counterbalance to the excessively object-focused mentality of our age, and it appears to centre consciousness that has become dispersed into myriad interests. Whether it is suitable for us in its ancient articulation, or whether it needs to be modified and adapted to present-day needs and a contemporary scientific understanding of the world, is a much discussed question.

All kinds of variants of Yoga have been developed, from ancient to modern times. The *Viṣṇu Purāṇa*, to mention just one such ancient adaptation, combines the steps of the *aṣṭāṅga yoga* with the worship of Viṣṇu. The Yogi is instructed to interiorize completely the image of Viṣṇu as it is traditionally represented: 'When this image never departs from his mind, whether he be going or standing, or engaged in any voluntary act, then he can consider his *dhāraṇa* (concentration) to be perfect.' A progressively more spiritual notion of Viṣṇu as 'self free from all distinction' leads to *samādhi* (trance). Along similar lines some contemporary authors have developed a 'Christian Yoga' which combines features of Patañjala Yoga with elements of Christian traditions.

Yoga has always had great importance for Hinduism. Even such philosophical systems as Vedānta, which disagree with Sāṁkhya-Yoga on matters of metaphysics, have incorporated Yoga into their practice. Recently a commentary on the *Yogasūtras* came to light which is ascribed to the great Advaitin Śaṅkara. While doubts about the authorship of the text persist, there is no question about the role which Yoga plays in the lives of Śaṅkara's adherents. It is an indispensable part of their preparatory training, and much of the theory and practice of Advaita Vedānta parallels the higher stages of Yoga, as we shall presently see.

Suggested further reading

Eliade, M. *Yoga: Immortality and Freedom*. Princeton University Press: Princeton, 1969.

Feuerstein, Georg. *The Philosophy of Classical Yoga*. University of Manchester Press: Manchester, 1982.

Koelman, G. M. *Patanjala Yoga: From Related Ego to Absolute Self*. Papal Athenaeum: Poona, 1970.

Taimni, I. K. *The Science of Yoga*. Theosophical Publishing House: Wheaton, Ill., 1972.

Govindaji Temple, Vṛīndāban, Uttar Pradesh

11

Śaṅkara and his Advaita Vedānta

Upaniṣadic thought, especially as systematized in Bādarāyaṇa's *Vedāntasūtras*, has remained the major inspiration for Hindu mysticism. Its variety and diversity carried over into the philosophical schools that developed over the centuries. The extremely elliptic *Vedāntasūtras*, containing about 550 aphorisms, often consisting of only a fragment of a sentence, require a commentary to make them understandable. Given the latitude of Hindu interpretation, the commentaries that were produced over the centuries vary widely. Thus, between the ninth and the fourteenth centuries ten recognized branches of Vedānta developed, each with its own *Brahmasūtrabhāṣya* (commentary), often enough augmented by *ṭīka* (subcommentaries).

It is obviously beyond the scope of this short introduction to give a description of all of them. Only a few will be introduced: Śaṅkara's Advaita Vedānta offers a non-theistic reading of the Vedāntic tradition. Rāmānuja's *Viśiṣṭa-Advaita*, Madhva's *Dvaita Vedānta* and Vallabha's *Puṣṭimārga* offer a theistic, Vaiṣṇava alternative interpretation.

In order to qualify as founder of a school of Vedānta, to be entitled to the name of 'Master' (*ācārya*), a religious leader had to compose commentaries on the major *Upaniṣads*, the *Bhagavadgītā* and the *Brahmasūtras*. Many, of course, wrote much more, and so an extensive, sophisticated literature developed, often in response to critique from other schools of thought.

The life and achievement of Śaṅkara

There is a major dispute about when Śaṅkara lived. While the majority of scholars accept 788–820 CE as his lifetime (some would have him born about a century earlier), a group of Hindus associated with a Śaṅkara *maṭha* in Kañcīpuram claims a pre-Buddhist period for the Ādiśaṅkarācārya, its founder. There is, however, common agreement that Śaṅkara considered it to be his life's work to consolidate Hinduism *vis-ā-vis* Buddhism, the dominant religion of the time, which by then was already on the wane in many parts of India.

Details of Śaṅkara's life have to be culled from several half-historical, half-legendary accounts of his victorious debating campaigns (*Digvijaya*), written by some of his disciples and later followers. According to these, Śaṅkara was born in Kālādī, Kerala, to Śivaguru and his wife Satī after they had prayed to Śiva for a son. Śivaguru died when Śaṅkara was only three. At five, he was sent to a *guru*'s home. Within two years he mastered the Vedas and the auxiliary literature, a study that normally takes twelve years. At a young age he desired to become a *samnyāsi*, an itinerant monk. His mother, entitled to refuse permission for her only son to renounce family-life, did not give in to his repeated entreaties. One day, however, while bathing, young Śaṅkara was caught by a crocodile. Threatened by death, he took the *samnyāsi* vow. According to Hindu tradition such a vow is valid. Miraculously, Śaṅkara escaped, and left home soon after. His *guru* was a sage, Govinda by name, living in the Narmadā forest. He is said to have been identical with Patañjali, the ancient teacher of Yoga and grammar. His reputed *guru*'s own teacher, Gauḍapada, however, seems to have exerted the greatest influence on Śaṅkara. Gauḍapada's exposition of the *Māṇḍūkya Upaniṣad*, the *Kārikās*, were the first and foremost text which Śaṅkara commented upon and made his own. His *guru* sent him to Banaras, since ancient times the major seat of Hindu learning. Śaṅkara soon established himself as a powerful exponent of *Advaita Vedānta*, the most radically monistic school of Hinduism.

A telling anecdote recounts how Śaṅkara, on his way to take his bath in the Ganges, met an outcaste accompanied by some dogs. Disgusted, he told him to go away. The man, however, began arguing with him, wondering on what basis he, who taught the identity of all things with *brahman*, made this distinction. Śaṅkara was embarrassed when the supposed sweeper revealed himself as Śiva, the great god. Śiva, however, blessed him and predicted Śaṅkara's greatness as teacher of Advaita Vedānta.

At the age of twelve Śaṅkara, according to tradition, composed his commentaries on the *Brahmasūtras*, the *Bhagavadgītā* and the *Upaniṣads*, as well as some other works. A total of seventy-two minor works, in addition to the major commentaries, are ascribed to him, including many hymns to Śiva, Viṣṇu and Devī. Having established himself as an *ācārya* ('Master'), he went on a *digvijaya* ('Victory Tour') through the length and breadth of India.

It is interesting to note that the main opponents he went to defeat were the *Mīmāṁsakas*, traditional vedic scholars, who held that the true Hindu tradition was circumscribed by vedic ritual and that the *Upaniṣads* were mere *arthavāda* (eulogy), words that did not form an essential part of religion. Their understanding of Hindu tradition was identical with the *karmamārga*, the performance of prescribed ritual acts. They had been successful in re-establishing Hinduism over against Buddhism. A major event in Śaṅkara's life was his debate with Maṇḍana Miśra, the foremost Mīmāṁsaka, which lasted for eighteen days. Maṇḍana Miśra's wife, herself a scholar, acted as umpire. In the end Maṇḍana Miśra declared himself convinced by Śaṅkara and became his disciple under the name of Sureśvara.

The traditional histories report a great many encounters with representatives of different schools of thought and sects then established in India. It is always Śaṅkara who wins the debates. He is as adept at countering stratagems and foul tricks as at defeating his opponents by logic and argument. He is credited with having renovated many temples, reorganized temple worship and, in general, with having renewed and reformed Hinduism. His most lasting contribution to living Hinduism, however, was his reputed establishment of monasteries (*maṭhas*) in the South, North, East and West of India and the organization of ten orders of monks (*daśanāmis*) associated with them. The *Śāradā Pītha* of Śriṅgerī in the South, the *Jyothi Maṭha* of Bādrinātha in the North, the *Kālikā Pīṭha* at Dvārakā in the West, and the *Vīmalā Pīṭha* in Jagannātha Puri in the East, are still centres of learning, and the respective heads of these, with the title of Śaṅkarācārya, enjoy a high reputation as religious leaders. Like their founder, the Ādiśaṅkarācārya, they spend much of their time travelling through their allotted districts, teaching and exhorting people to practise their religion. The Daśanāmi *saṁnyāsis*, who have to undergo a rigorous training before initiation, count at present only a few hundred, but are highly respected throughout India. While in the West Śaṅkara's fame rests on his philosophy – by many he is regarded the greatest of India's thinkers – in India itself his major contribution is seen in his practical achievements in consolidating and reforming Hinduism.

Śaṅkara, according to tradition, died at the young age of thirty-two and was buried at Kāñcīpuram, which also became a major *maṭha* presided over by a Śaṅkarācārya.

Advaita Vedānta as philosophy

Śaṅkara, like all other Hindu thinkers, does not claim originality for his thought but considers it the correct exposition and interpretation of *śruti*, revealed truth. Nevertheless, ideas that are unmistakably his became the focus of disputes with other schools. One of these ideas is the notion of *adhyāsa* (superimposition).

Śaṅkara maintains that all subject/object knowledge is distorted by it: we habitually superimpose objective notions on the subject, and subjective notions on the object. Since this *adhyāsa* is congenital, we are not even aware of it. In order to know truth as such, however, we have to overcome it. Śaṅkara uses the familiar illustration of the traveller who mistakes a piece of rope for a snake, or a snake for a piece of rope. Śaṅkara concludes that all knowledge acquired through the senses is ambiguous and cannot be used to arrive at certain truth. However, the existence of the thinking subject is not to be doubted. Every perception, be it right, wrong or ambiguous, needs a perceiver, distinct from all objects perceived. The *ātman*, the subject proper, is pure consciousness, different from all objects and all sense-organs, including *manas*, the rational mind. *Ātman* finally emerges as the only reality, identical with *brahman*, characterized only by *sat* (being), *cit* (consciousness) and *ānanda* (bliss).

Śaṅkara does not consider the world a pure illusion, as is sometimes maintained; he condemns the Buddhist idealists, for whom everything is *śūnyatā*, emptiness. He only looks at it from the standpoint of absolute being. If *brahman*, which is eternal, self-sufficient, pure consciousness, is the measure of reality, then the phenomenal world, which is evanescent, changing, devoid of consciousness, cannot be called real in the same sense. It is the congenital *avidyā* (ignorance) that superimposes features of *brahman* on the world of senses, and features of things on the Absolute. To gain *vidyā* (knowledge) means to recognize this situation and to understand *brahman* and the world on their own terms. If ignorance of the true nature of reality keeps us in *saṁsāra*, the round of births and deaths and the world of becoming, true knowledge will emancipate us from it.

Śaṅkara sees in the Great Sayings of the *Upaniṣads* the expression of revealed, liberating truth. Their common message is that *ātman* is *brahman*, which means that the individual self is no different from the ground of being. *Brahman*, by its very nature, is imperceptible by the senses and is not identical with any object. Śaṅkara quotes Upaniṣadic passages which speak of a 'lower' and a 'higher' *brahman*. He interprets the 'lower *brahman*' to mean *īśvara*, the God of religion, who is worshipped as creator, sustainer and destroyer of this world. The 'higher *brahman*' he understands to be the quality-less, acosmic principle of all.

This is the source of his controversial distinction between a *saguṇa* and a *nirguṇa brahman*, an Ultimate with and without qualities. For Śaṅkara, the creator-god, *īśvara*, is essentially connected with his creation. With the dissolution of the universe he too disappears, whereas *brahman*, understood as *nirguṇa*, remains forever. Śaṅkara is known as composer of various popular hymns in praise of Viṣṇu, Śiva and Devī. For him, devotion to *īśvara* is a necessary stage on the way to emancipation, not an end in itself.

The process that alone leads to emancipation from *saṁsāra* and a complete merging of the individual *ātman* with the universal *brahman* is called *viveka*, discernment. There is a short text ascribed to Śaṅkara, the *Vivekacūḍāmanī* ('Crestjewel of Discernment'), which teaches methodically how to differentiate between the Self and the not-Self. It states: 'There is no *avidyā* (ignorance) outside the mind. Mind alone is *avidyā*, the cause of the bondage of transmigration. When that is destroyed, all else is destroyed, and when it is manifested, everything else is manifested. The mind is the only cause that brings about a person's bondage or liberation.' And further: 'This bondage can be destroyed neither by weapons, nor by wind, nor by fire, nor by millions of actions – by nothing except the wonderful sword of knowledge that comes from discernment, sharpened by the grace of the Lord.'

Śaṅkara's philosophy has been called *Māyāvāda* ('Illusionism'), especially by his opponents, who resisted the equation of the phenomenal universe with *māyā* (illusion). Śaṅkara, however, does not simply declare the world an illusion. He distinguishes between two modes of knowing: *vyavahārika* and *paramārthika*: knowledge derived from a pragmatic, worldly perspective, and knowledge gained from an ultimate, transcendent point of view. From a pragmatic perspective the world is as real for Śaṅkara as for anybody else: one has to accept the reality of the world if one wishes to undertake any action whatsoever. However, and this is Śaṅkara's point, that is not the only way one can look at it. Someone who has intuitively understood the nature of *ātman/brahman* can no longer equate reality with the everchanging, transient world. Only to persons who have reached that level of enlightenment, who are able to see it from the viewpoint of eternity, will the world appear as *māyā*, 'unreal'.

PREREQUISITES FOR THE STUDY OF VEDĀNTA

The study of *dharma* results in transitory heaven and this depends on the performance of rituals. The inquiry into the nature of *brahman*, however, results in liberation. It does not depend on the performance of ceremonies.

These are the preconditions for the inquiry into the nature of *brahman*:

1. discernment between the eternal and the non-eternal
2. renunciation of all enjoyment of the fruit of one's actions both here and hereafter
3. practice of the standard virtues such as peaceableness, self-restraint, etc.
4. overriding desire for liberation.

The object of desire is the knowledge of *brahman* and complete understanding of it. Knowledge is therefore the means to perfect *brahman* cognition. The complete knowledge of *brahman* is the supreme goal of humans, because it destroys the root of all evil, namely ignorance, which is the seed of transmigration.

Śaṅkara, *Brahmasūtrabhāṣya* I, 1, 1.

Advaita Vedānta as religion

While, generally speaking, traditional India did not distinguish between philosophy and religion the way this is done in the West, from our own perspective we can do so. The issues dealt with in the preceding section may be termed 'philosophical'. They represent an attempt rationally and speculatively to explore the nature of reality. As became clear from the brief biographical sketch, Śaṅkara was not only a philosopher, but also – and principally – a religious reformer. Śaṅkara never leaves any doubt that he grounds his *darśaṇa*, his worldview, not on reason, but on *śruti*, revelation. Only the *Upaniṣads* lead to *brahmavidyā*, the knowledge of the highest; only the insight gained from an understanding of the *mahāvākyas*, the Great Saying of the *Upaniṣads*, brings liberation. Śaṅkara also says that one of the preconditions of the study of Vedānta is faith (*śraddhā*) and he recommends devotion (*bhakti*) to God in order ultimately to realize *brahman*. The attainment of *mokṣa* (liberation) is not a matter of one's own effort alone, but also of divine grace. The very goal to be reached is religious: it is not a sensual paradise or a gain of empirical knowledge, but a total identification with the quality-less reality called *brahman*.

Already during his lifetime Śaṅkara's disciples considered his words to be on a par with divine revelation and he himself, regarded by many as an incarnation of Śiva, was treated as an embodiment of divine wisdom. Śaṅkara's tradition, his philosophy as well as his religion, has continued right up to our time. Many scholars have studied his works and written books in defence of his thought. A galaxy of famous names in the history of Hinduism – Sureśvara, Padmapada, Vācaspati Miśra, Madhusūdhana Sarasvatī, Vīdyāraṇya, to name but a few – have, in the centuries following Śaṅkara, refined Advaita Vedānta and defended it against rival systems. One particularly ingenious defence deserves mention. In his *Sarvadarśanasaṁgraha*, a survey of all philosophical systems, Mādhava, a fourteenth-century Advaitin, presents a total of sixteen different schools of thought. Beginning with the *Cārvākas*, crude materialists, who by common consent are at the bottom of the ladder, he lets each school be refuted by the next. The last system presented, of course, is Advaita Vedānta, which, after all the other schools have successively annulled each other, shines forth as the final statement of truth.

In today's India, many academic philosophers would call themselves Advaitins: Sarvepalli Radhakrishnan, the President of India from 1962 to 1967, and perhaps the most widely known contemporary representative of Indian thought, was an Advaitin. T. R.V. Murti, S. K. Maitra, T. M. P. Mahadevan, major luminaries in twentieth-century Indian philosophy, were Advaitins. Mahadevan, in particular, virtually established in the Department of Philosophy at the University of Madras, and in the Centre for Advanced Research in Philosophy, a new school of Advaita Vedānta. Under his leadership many Advaitic texts were edited and translated, and he personally kept in close touch with the Śaṅkarācārya of Kāñcīpuram, about whom he spoke and wrote with great reverence. He was a very religious person, devoting, especially towards the end of his life, a great amount of his time to meditation and worship. He not only wrote learned monographs on Advaita and Advaitins, but also translated and commented on the religious hymns ascribed to Śaṅkara.

Today's Śaṅkarācāryas, the heads of the monasteries established by Śaṅkara, are highly respected religious authorities. Each *maṭha*, the headquarters of one or more orders of monks, not only has a school which cultivates traditional learning and especially the study of Advaita Vedānta, but also has a temple where regular service is performed, and which serves as a place of pilgrimage for thousands, who may have little knowledge of Advaita Vedānta as a philosophy.

Advaita Vedānta has also attracted Western thinkers. While in the nineteenth century many found it of interest because they saw in it a kind of Indian Hegelianism, more recent and more adequate readings of Advaita appreciate it for its own sake. Thus Erwin Schrödinger, a Nobel-prizewinning physicist, offers in his writings a quasi-empirical proof for Vedānta, exemplified in the unity of knower, known and knowledge. He did not think it possible that this unity of knowledge, feeling and choice which one calls one's own should have come from nothingness just now. He was convinced that this knowledge, feeling and choice were 'essentially eternal and unchangeable and numerically one in all humans, nay in all sensitive beings'. Schrödinger, as a contemporary man, was haunted by the question 'What is Real?' and as a nuclear physicist he was no longer prepared to equate the real with the empirical. After all, even in today's physics there is nothing to be seen or touched once the subatomic barrier has been crossed. The 'unseen' has in a very convincing manner turned out to be the source of the 'seen' – a twentieth-century verification of Uddālaka's teaching, illustrated several thousand years ago by a fig and its seeds. *Tat tvam asi*, 'That are you', said Uddālaka to his son Śvetaketu. To find our true identity remains the great task for all of us.

Suggested further reading

Cenkner, William. *A Tradition of Teachers: Shankara and the Jagadgurus Today*. Motilal Banarsidass: Delhi, 1983.

Deutsch, Elliot. *Advaita Vedānta: A Philosophical Reconstruction*. University of Hawaii: Honolulu, 1969.

Deutsch, Elliot and J. A. B. van Buitenen (eds.). *A Source Book of Advaita Vedanta*. University of Hawaii: Honolulu, 1971.

Murty, K. S. *Revelation and Reason in Advaita Vedanta*. Waltair University: Waltair, 1961.

12
Vaiṣṇava theistic Vedānta

Rightly or wrongly Śaṅkara's Advaita Vedānta was perceived by many as undermining the Hindu tradition. He was accused of being a 'Crypto-Buddhist', smuggling notions of Buddhist 'emptiness' into Hinduism via his teaching on *māyā*, the illusory nature of the world. His distinction between a 'higher' and a 'lower' *brahman*, and his identification of the latter with the Lord worshipped by the pious as creator, sustainer and redeemer, offended many Hindus. That he apparently negated the reality of the universe, and relativized the importance of scriptures and teachers, was also held against him. In an India in which Hinduism had no longer to fight for its survival against Buddhists and Jains and a host of other unorthodox religions, Hindus could return to working out the systematics of their own traditions and engaging in debate among themselves. While Vedānta as systematized in the *Brahmasūtras* remained normative, and while it also remained understood that the *Bhagavadgītā* and the *Upaniṣads* were authoritative proof-texts, many, especially in the Vaiṣṇava community, not only claimed the status of revealed scripture for other writings, like the *Viṣṇu Purāṇa* or the *Bhāgavata Purāṇa*, but also held that Śaṅkara's interpretations were flawed. This is the background to the emergence of the school of *Śrīvaiṣṇavism*, whose most prominent exponent was Rāmānuja.

Gopura at entrance to Tirupati shrine

The ācāryas of Śrīraṅgam

Śrīraṅgam is a holy city built on an island in the river Kāverī, not far from the modern city of Tiruchirapalli in Tamilnadu, South India. It is not only one of the most popular destinations for pilgrims from all over India, but also the seat of the 'pope' of the community of Śrīvaiṣṇavas. The first of these was Nāṭha Muni, who lived in the ninth century CE. He accepted the Tamil *Prabandham*, the collection of hymns by the Āḷvārs (a group of inspired religious poets living between the sixth and ninth centuries in the Tamil country), as equal to scripture. That meant that their songs could be used in formal temple worship and that their expressions of faith were given highest authority. The *Pāñcarātra* worship tradition which Nāṭha Muni had inherited from his father, together with the devotion of the *Āḷvārs* and the more scholastic Vedānta, became the foundation for the future Śrīvaiṣṇavism. Nāṭha Muni was succeeded by his grandson, Yamuna, a scholar who wrote several important works that helped to consolidate Vaiṣṇava Vedānta. Rāmānuja (1017–1137 CE), called to Yamunācārya's deathbed, promised to fulfil his three unfulfilled dying wishes: to honour the memory of the sages Vyāsa and Parāśara, the authors of the *Viṣṇu Purāṇa;* to keep alive the hymns of Nammāḷvār, the greatest of the Āḷvārs; and to write a commentary on the *Brahmasūtras* from a Vaiṣṇava standpoint.

Taking over the headship of Śrīraṅgam, Rāmānuja introduced many reforms and reorganized its worship. Apparently some of the temple priests did not find the changes to their liking and tried to poison him. Rāmānuja, however, prevailed and gained control of the community. He succeeded in establishing Śrīvaiṣṇavism in Tirupati, an ancient and famous place of pilgrimage in today's Andhra Pradesh, reputedly the richest temple in India.

The expanding activities on behalf of the Vaiṣṇava community were rudely interrupted by a persecution, instigated by an intolerant Śaivite king. Rāmānuja fled to the neighbouring kingdom of

Mysore, whose ruler became his disciple. The latter built a temple at Melkote, where Rāmānuja spent twelve years, waiting out the persecution in the Chola country. On returning to Śrīraṅgam he met again with his faithful servant, Kureśa, whose eyes had been plucked out by the Śaivites because he had refused to betray his faith in Viṣṇu. Rāmānuja's tears restored Kureśa's sight. According to traditional accounts, Rāmānuja died at the venerable age of 120, bewailed by a large community of faithful Vaiṣṇavas.

While Śrīvaiṣṇava sources mix and mingle legend and history, it is beyond doubt that Rāmānuja shaped Śrīvaiṣṇavism decisively. He not only provided it with the authoritative commentary to the *Brahmasūtra* and other writings that articulated a Vaiṣṇava Vedānta, but he also determined the mode of worship in Vaiṣṇava temples and established the Śrīraṅgam *ācāryas*, the heads of the school, as the highest authority in matters of doctrine and practice.

Today's Śrīvaiṣṇava community, being fairly large, is divided into Teṅgalais ('Southerners'), with their centre at Śrīraṅgam, and Vaḍagalais ('Northerners'), for whom Kāñcīpuram has remained the seat. The split developed in the fourteenth century over linguistic as well as doctrinal issues. The Northerners preferred Sanskrit sources, while the Southerners insisted on the equal authority of Sanskrit and Tamil. Also, the Teṅgalais, later known as the 'cat school', believed that, as a cat carries its kitten out of a fire by the scruff of its neck, so God saves without human cooperation. The Vaḍagalais, the 'monkey school', likened the process of salvation to the way young monkeys cling to their mothers when carried away from a fire. God, according to this school, requires a person's active involvement in the process of salvation.

Viśiṣṭa Advaita: the teaching of Rāmānuja

The technical designation of the form of Vedānta developed by the Śrīraṅgam *ācāryas* is *Viśiṣta Advaita*, 'Qualified Advaita'. While

RĀMĀNUJA'S DESCRIPTION OF GOD

He shines like a huge mountain of molten gold. He possesses the radiance of a hundred thousand suns. His eyes are like the petals of a lotus in the early morning sun. His face is utterly charming. His coral-like lips are smiling. His arms are strong, his waist is slender, and his chest is broad. All parts of his person are well proportioned. The exquisite harmony of his features is beyond description. His feet are like two lotus flowers. His golden garment fits perfectly. He is adorned with many marvellous ornaments.

He has charmed the hearts of all by his exceedingly attractive beauty. His all-pervasive loveliness fills and overflows all beings. His eternal youthfulness is absolutely marvellous. He possesses the freshness of blossoms. The endless vastness of the universe is filled with his fragrance. He shines in majesty throughout the three worlds. He looks at his devotees with compassion, love and graciousness. He is the very opposite of everything evil. He is an ocean of auspicious attributes. He is the supreme Brahman, the highest Self, Nārāyaṇa.

Rāmānuja, *Vedārthasaṅgraha*, No. 220

accepting a fundamental likeness between humans and the Supreme God, they wanted to see it 'qualified' in a variety of ways. To begin with, Viṣṇu, identical with the *brahman* of the *Upaniṣads*, is creator, sustainer and redeemer. He is distinguished from all others by his transcendental qualities, such as omnipotence and gracefulness. The universe, far from being *māyā*, illusory appearance, is God's body. The relationship between humans and their God is circumscribed by notions such as *śeṣa-śeṣī-bhāva*, or *aṁśa-aṁśī-bhāva*, meaning that whereas God is absolute, humans are contingent on him, and whereas God is the whole, humans are only parts. While the original nature of human beings had been pure and blissful, due to certain limitations, they became entangled in *saṁsāra*, and thereby unhappy.

Rāmānuja speaks about the 'forgetfulness' of human beings, which makes them mistake their own identity. He illustrates the human condition with a well-known parable: a young prince, while playing outside his father's palace, got lost in the adjacent jungle. A compassionate forester took him into his home and brought him up. He grew up with the other children, as one of the forester's sons. One day a courtier happened to come by and, recognizing the lost prince, told him that his father had been anxiously searching for him ever since his disappearance. Immediately the young prince recognized the truth of what the messenger was saying, and prepared to meet his real father. The King, hearing of the discovery of his long-lost son, went halfway to meet him with a retinue of servants. Embracing him warmly, he conducted him in procession to his palace amidst the rejoicing of the entire city.

The meaning of the parable is clear: the soul, getting lost in *saṁsāra*, the world of the senses, and dwelling with worldly people, forgets her divine origin. Reminded by a trustworthy person, a *guru*, of her true nature, she remembers it instantly and longs to return to her origin. God, waiting for the soul to come back, welcomes her and blesses her with his presence.

As the name *Śrīvaiṣṇavism* indicates, in Rāmānuja's theology Śrī, the consort of Viṣṇu, plays a major role. She is called 'Mother of the Universe' and is eternal and inseparable from Viṣṇu. She is omnipresent like Viṣṇu, and assumes a form corresponding to that in which Viṣṇu appears: as a god, a human, or an animal. Śrī also plays a major role in the salvation of people. In later developments, such as Caitaṇya's *Gauḍīya Vaiṣṇavism* and Nīmbārka's *Puṣṭimārga*, Śrī's role is increased to the point where she becomes more important than Viṣṇu, and salvation is ascribed mainly to her graceful intervention.

Similarly, the role of the *guru* is central to Vaiṣṇavism. Rāmānuja holds that the *guru* is indispensable. Śrī is the first and foremost of *gurus*, mediator between humankind and God. She is the embodiment of grace and mercy, whose endeavours win the blessing of God. She is the model for the human *guru*, who should be entirely free of selfishness and, desirous of the welfare of others, must not be motivated by profit or fame. Later Vaiṣṇava systems again exaggerate the role of the *guru* to the point where he becomes more important than God. As the saying goes: 'If God is angry with a person, she can go to the *guru* and have the *guru* intercede on her behalf. If the *guru* is angry, there is no refuge left for the disciple.'

Anti-advaita polemics

A great deal of Rāmānuja's and the later Vaiṣṇavas' writings is concerned with polemics against Śaṅkara and his Advaita Vedānta. To begin with, Rāmānuja states that there is no scriptural basis for either superimposition (*adhyāsa*) or a Supreme Being without qualities (*nirguṇa brahman*). The quotes from the *Upaniṣads* which Śaṅkara uses to prove his point do not speak of a quality-less being but indicate only the absence of all evil in *brahman*. Rāmānuja says that scripture reveals a Supreme Person (*puruṣottama*) whose nature is absolute bliss and goodness, who is fundamentally averse to all evil. He is different from all beings, and the cause of the creation, sustenance and dissolution of the world. For Rāmānuja *brahman*, the Absolute Being, and *īśvara*, the Lord of Creation, are one and the same. Similarly, while Śaṅkara holds that liberation consists only in shedding wrong notions, a basic insight into the nature of reality, Rāmānuja sees it as a cumulative process of acquiring merit and grace, worshipping and serving God for a lifetime, and becoming god-like. The ultimate condition for Rāmānuja does not mean merging without trace into the impersonal *brahman*. He believes that the released will be endowed with an incorruptible body similar to that of Viṣṇu, sharing Viṣṇu's heaven, Vaikuṇṭha, with the celestial beings and all the other released souls.

Madhva's *Dvaita Vedānta*

Madhva (1238–1317 CE), born into a humble Brahmin family in a village not far from Uḍipī, in today's Karṇāṭaka state, first became the disciple of Acutyaprekṣa, a teacher of Advaita Vedānta. Disagreeing with him frequently, he nevertheless won his respect and was installed by him as the head of the monastery, being given the name Ānandatīrtha. He accused Rāmānuja of compromising too much with Advaita, and sought to establish the most radical opposition to Śaṅkara, calling his own system *Dvaita Vedānta*, 'dualistic' Vedānta, and beginning by enumerating five radical differences between human beings and the Ultimate: finite living beings are radically distinct from inert matter, as well as from the infinite *brahman*, and they differ among themselves as well. The essential God-human relationship is expressed in the term *biṁba-Pratibiṁba*, image and reflection. God is the prototype, and all human beings are like reflections, shadows of the Ultimate. Bondage is due to ignorance, but it is only through God's grace that one can be released.

Madhva is unique in assuming that a whole group of people is predestined never to be released and to be bound forever. Viṣṇu alone is Lord, source of everything, from whom all knowledge flows and who both binds and releases human beings. *Bhakti*, the love of God, is the means to winning God's grace: it leads to *sākṣātkāra*, a bodily vision of God. When enjoying God's bliss in heaven, souls depend on God and they also differ from each other in the degree of their bliss. As vessels of different sizes can all be 'full' but contain different amounts of water, so each soul receives bliss according to her capacity. So complete is the transformation that, as Madhva states, 'the released takes everything with the hands of God, sees only through the eyes of God, walks with the feet of God'.

Madhva was the most prolific writer among the major Vedāntins, and he also ranged wider in his use of sources. He accepted the Vaiṣṇava *Purāṇas* and *Saṁhitās* as scriptures, and wrote commentaries on the *Ṛgveda* and parts of the *Mahābhārata*. He was also the most aggressive defender of Viṣṇu's glory, and he was feared in his lifetime by his opponents. He is said to have persuaded a contemporary king to have thousands of Jains impaled for refusing to accept Vaiṣṇavism. He claimed to be the *avatāra*, the human appearance of Vāyu, the wind-god, 'the holy spirit', and he demanded that his followers, to express their unwavering dedication to Viṣṇu, have their bodies branded with the symbols of Viṣṇu.

Vallabha's *puṣṭimārga*

Vallabha (1481–1533 CE), a Telugu brahmin, originally affiliated with the school of Viṣṇusvāmi, became the founder of another school of Vaiṣṇava Vedānta, which became known as *puṣṭimārga*, literally 'the way of nourishment', or way of grace. He elevated the *Bhāgavata Purāṇa* to the highest grade of scripture: for him it was the only authentic commentary on the *Brahmasūtras*. Convinced that in his time the *saṁnyāsa* ideal had deteriorated beyond repair, he emphasized the virtues of family life and the importance of worship performed in a family setting. He endeavoured to distinguish his school not only from Advaita but also from the other *bhakti* schools. The centre of his teaching, *puṣṭi*, is the uncaused grace of God for which devotees prepare, but which they will never be able to influence. Vallabha thinks it impossible to state the reason for God's pleasure, according to which he extends his grace; suffering cannot be the reason, because there are many sufferers who do not receive his grace. The *puṣṭimārga* is liberal, admitting women and children and even 'fallen' people, meaning persons of low castes and those to whom other schools of thought can offer no hope. The great models of lovers of God are the *gopīs* of Vṛndāban, the milkmaids who followed Kṛṣṇa, disregarding their own fate and reputation.

Vallabha makes a distinction between *mokṣa*, Vedāntic liberation, and *nityā līlā*, eternal love-play, the ultimate aim of his own sect. While not denying the possibility of *mokṣa*, the permanent enjoyment of God's company seems to him preferable by far. Vallabha assumes that love of God is innate in all humans, but that it has to be cultivated and nourished. As regards the worship of the God image, which is as central to the *puṣṭimārga* as to all other branches of Vaiṣṇavism, Vallabha distinguishes between *sevā* (service), and *pūjā* (worship). Only the worship of Śrī Govardhānanāṭha, also called Nāṭhajī, the image of the deity revealed to Vallabha on the hill of Girirāja, qualifies as *sevā*. All forms of worship offered to other manifestations of the deity are *pūjā*, directed to appearances of the Lord, not to his real presence. Vallabha emphasizes the sovereignty of God more than others. Those whom God has chosen attain an almost god-like state; those whom he does not choose will remain in *saṁsāra*, the cycle of birth and death, forever.

A trend towards devotionalism

Vaiṣṇavism has always had a tendency to develop ever new forms and schools of thought. It is therefore not possible within the context of this beginner's guide to deal with all of them. While all Vaiṣṇavas were interested in belonging to the vedāntic tradition, which conveys theological respectability and recognition, for many Vaiṣṇava communities the vedāntic, intellectual element became less and less important in relation to the intuitions of particular *gurus*, ceremonial worship and inspirational *bhakti* literature. Vaiṣṇava religious energy, from the fifteenth century on, did not go into writing commentaries on the vedāntic classics, but into developing elaborate codes of worship and producing poetic effusions in honour of the manifestations of Viṣṇu. The hymns, sometimes of considerable length, are not devoid of metaphysical depth, but their tenor is worshipful, not argumentative. In our day and age Vaiṣṇava Vedānta is alive and well in the hands of a number of experts. However, the majority of people are drawn towards it not so much because it is intellectually superior to other schools of thought, but because it maintains popular places of pilgrimage, celebrates important festivals, and satisfies the longings of the heart.

Suggested further reading

Carman, John Braistead. *The Theology of Ramanuja*. Yale University Press: New Haven, Conn., 1974.

Lipner, Julius. *The face of Truth: A Study of Meaning and Metaphysics in the Vedantic Theology of Ramanuja*. Macmillan: London, 1986.

Sarma, B. N. K. *Madhva's Teachings in His Own Words*. Bharatiya Vidya Bhavan: Bombay, 1961.

Yamunacarya, M. *Ramanuja's Teachings in His Own Words*. Bharatiya Vidya Bhavan: Bombay, 1963.

Part IV
Hinduism Encounters Other Religions

With the great diversity of its expressions Hinduism has always had to operate in a pluralistic situation. This impression is reinforced by the multiplicity of breakaway religions that established themselves as competitors, such as Buddhism and Jainism (not to mention historically important but now defunct movements like the Ajīvikas and others), which for some time threatened fully to eclipse traditional Hinduism. That Hindus were aware of the challenges of religious pluralism is amply borne out by scholarly Hindu literature from at least the seventh century CE onwards: Kumārila Bhaṭṭa, a prominent representative of *Pūrva Mīmāṁsā*, in his *Ślokavārttika* (a commentary on the first part of the *Mīmāṁsāsūtra*), extensively refers to, and polemicizes against, several Buddhist schools. The Buddhists, of course, took up the challenge: Śāntarakṣita, in his voluminous *Tattvasaṁgraha*, quotes extensively from the *Ślokavārttika* in order to refute it, together with other schools of Hinduism. From then on it became customary for every scholarly work first to describe and refute opposing schools of thought – non-Hindu as well as Hindu – before giving a detailed account of its own position. Thus the fourteenth century Mādhava, in his *Sarvadarśanasaṁgraha*, not only relates and critiques the unorthodox Cārvākas, Buddhists and Jains, but also mentions and rejects Rāmānuja's Śrīvaiṣṇavism, Nakuliśa's Pāśupata Śaivism, Jaimini's Mīmāṁsā, Gautama's Nyāya, Paṇini's Yoga. He further argues against many others who are in (partial) disagreement with his own Advaita Vedānta, which he presents as the crown of Hinduism.

Temple elephant at procession

Polemics and criticism of rival systems became a universal practice for Hindu scholars – one which is continued to this very day.

While rivalry among Hindu schools of thought and breakaway systems was usually restricted to debate and argumentation (very rarely do we hear of attempts to convert adherents of other communities by force, or of persecution of dissenters), the situation changed dramatically with the advent of Islam in India. The Muslim invaders saw it as an expression of their faith to conquer the infidels' lands and convert them to Islam. While, according to Islamic law, nobody should be forced to become a Muslim, in practice considerable pressure was applied. Muslims found Hindu 'idolatry' especially repulsive, and destroyed and plundered literally thousands of Hindu temples from the eleventh century onwards, as testified by their own historians, who gloried in those exploits. Millions of Hindus, especially from the lower classes, became Muslims. In later centuries, notably under some of the more open-minded Mughal emperors like Akbar, Hindus were not only left in peace but even occupied important positions at court. Yet Muslims were clearly favoured, and Hindus as a religious community felt under siege. It was largely due to this situation that Hinduism became rigid and withdrawn, developing a xenophobic character.

Hindu-Muslim conflicts, as is well known, have periodically ravaged Indian villages and towns, and the seemingly irreconcilable differences between Hinduism and Islam led to the partition of India in 1947 into the Muslim-dominated Pakistan and the predominantly Hindu Bhārat, or India. Problems persist, as major Hindu-Muslim conflagrations in 1982/3 and 1992/3 have demonstrated.

With the discovery of a sea route to India by Vasco da Gama in 1498 and the subsequent conquest of India by European nations, a new chapter in the encounter between Hinduism and other religions began: that of Christian missions. Portugal, the first Western power to conquer and occupy territory in India, soon began to Christianize Goa, in mid-western India. It offered the inhabitants of Goa the choice between converting or leaving their homeland. Hindu temples were destroyed and Christianity, as practised in Portugal at that time, became the only permissible religion. Portuguese missionaries were also sent to other areas of India where they claimed to have baptized tens of thousands of 'heathen'. Their reports of Hinduism, with few exceptions, were filled with negative comments and expressions of contempt. More enlightened missionaries, like de Nobili, realized that the interest which the brahmins cultivated in things spiritual, was an asset also to Christianity. They tried against much opposition – which eventually prevailed – to assimilate Christian worship into Hindu culture in certain respects.

The other European countries that eventually established colonies in India – Denmark, France and especially Britain – were less bigoted: they were satisfied with Christian preachers operating in their territories, often with considerable restrictions. They had come to India first and foremost to trade, and religious concerns were not to interfere with business. When Britain, in 1808, became virtually the ruler of most of India – a situation that was officially acknowledged when the British Crown took control of the country in 1857 – Christian (especially Protestant) missionary activity among the Hindus became a major effort. Missionaries opened schools, built churches, translated the scriptures into Indian languages, gathered congregations of converts. There clearly was some advantage in becoming Christian in those times, and the number of Christians grew steadily.

Hinduism's encounter with Christianity, however, was not a one-way street: some Hindus, without converting to Christianity, but appreciating what they saw in the foreign missionaries, began rethinking their own tradition. Thus Raja Ram Mohan Roy (1772–1833), an open-minded Brahmin from Bengal, not only entered into an exchange with William Carey, a British missionary stationed in the Danish enclave Serampore (Śrīrāmpura), but also tried to incorporate features of Christianity which he found appealing into his own religion. He eventually, in 1828, founded the Brahmo Sabhā, a new religious movement, in which Hindu and Christian elements were blended. After initial success it eventually declined, largely due to the peculiarities of some of its leaders.

Christian missions in India also provoked strong opposition: many Hindus felt the new religion a threat to their own tradition, especially since it was the religion of the foreign power that had forcibly occupied India. Hindu resistance against Christianity found expression in many forms and was voiced by many Indians. No one did this as forcefully and successfully as Dayananda Saraswati, who eventually founded the Ārya Samāj. His initiative spawned a host of others that are still very much alive today.

When India gained independence in 1947, Hindus were free to take charge of their own affairs. Hinduism underwent a renaissance and also became increasingly politicized. In today's India Hinduism is not only the vigorous and visible religion of the majority of the people, but also a major political force, regionally and nationally.

In the following we shall deal only with the results of the encounter between Hinduism and the modern West. Interesting as the older encounters between Hinduism, Buddhism and other heterodox religions have been, it is the more recent developments that affect India's present and future the most.

13

Hinduism welcomes modern Western ideas

During the second half of the eighteenth century the once glorious Moghul Empire of India, admired by sixteenth-century European travellers as the richest and most populous on earth, was collapsing. Much of its territory was already under the control of foreign powers, and the rest was left to the whims of local potentates and bands of robbers. People were starving, the roads were insecure, laws no longer seemed to exist. Hinduism, too, was in a most pitiable state. Superstition and moral decay, ignorance and neglect of places of worship were the features most noticed by contemporary observers. Many observers considered Hinduism hopelessly moribund and expected it to succumb within decades to the process of degeneration. Many, including Indians themselves, saw India's future in westernization, if not Christianization. The prosperity of newly industrializing Western countries was contrasted with India's poverty, and as the West's success was attributed to its religion so was India's sorry condition linked to Hinduism. It was seen not only as weak and decaying, but also as incapable of reform and renewal. Yet India, once again, proved its doomsayers wrong.

The first stirrings of Hindu reform: Ram Mohan Roy (1772–1833) and the Brahmo Samāj

The British East India Company, founded in 1600 to promote trade, eventually took control of most of Bengal, and developed

Calcutta into a major city. Initially it banned all missionary activity in its territory, and its contacts with the people of Bengal were strictly regulated by business. However, it soon began recruiting and training locals for its service. To associate with foreigners, to learn a *mleccha* ('barbaric') language, to wear non-Indian dress, required some adventurousness on the part of Hindus, and many considered it incompatible with Hindu custom.

Ram Mohan Roy, one of the first Hindus to enter the Company's service, was a rebel: after a period of study at the Muslim university in Patna, during which he developed a serious interest in Sufism, he turned against image worship and fell out with his Vaiṣṇava father. He gave up his position with the East India Company in order to devote himself to religious studies. He then intended to reform Hinduism by returning to the sources, the *Upaniṣads*. Establishing contact with the English missionaries who had opened a college at Serampore, a Danish enclave near Calcutta, he began studying Greek and Hebrew in order to translate the Bible into Bengali. He was attracted by what he read, and wrote a pamphlet entitled *The Precepts of Jesus: The Guide to Peace and Happiness*. The results were unexpected: his Hindu friends accused him of making propaganda for Christianity, the Christian missionaries resented his 'Hinduizing of Jesus'. He accused the missionaries of misinterpreting the words of Jesus – a charge that Hindus continue to make.

Several times Ram Mohan Roy attempted to found an association of like-minded Hindus who shared his ideas of religion: a blend of Upaniṣadic wisdom and Gospel ethics. He eventually succeeded in 1828 with his 'Brahmo Sabhā', the 'assembly of devotees of the supreme brahman', gathering a small group of reform-minded Hindus. Although he intended to remain a Hindu, keeping his sacred thread and observing some Hindu ritual, many in the Hindu community considered him a traitor and excluded him.

Convinced of the value of modern scientific education, Ram Mohan Roy also promoted the establishment of English schools in

Calcutta. His greatest triumph, however, was the abolition of *satī*, the burning of mostly young wives on their dead husbands' funeral pyres. For this cause he fought for ten years after witnessing the forced *satī* of a dear relation, and making it his life's goal to see the cruel custom outlawed. Against the opposition of traditional Hindus, who maintained that *satī* was part of Hindu religious practice, with which the British had vowed not to interfere, he succeeded. He died in 1833 in England while fighting the appeal which the orthodox had launched against the decision, and was buried in Bristol.

The Brahmo Sabhā, later reorganized in 1843, and renamed 'Brahmo Samāj' by Debendranath Tagore, called a 'Hindu Protestantism' by contemporary observers, repudiated much of popular Hindu belief and practice. It taught a monotheism, rejected image worship, dissociated itself from puranic mythology, and insisted on a rather puritan ethic. Its scriptures were the *Upaniṣads* and those sections of works like the *Mahābhārata* which preached a high ethical ideal. Ram Mohan Roy wished to wed the metaphysics of the Vedānta with the ethics of the Gospels. Many foreign observers thought that the Brahmo Samāj could become the future religion of India; none of the objectionable features of Hinduism were to be found in it.

While Ram Mohan Roy remained sympathetic to Christianity, his successor, Debendranath Tagore, called *Maharsi*, took a decidedly anti-missionary line. He founded a Bengali newspaper and a school for Brahmo missionaries, with the explicit purpose of checking the spread of Christianity in India. He also broke with Hindu orthodoxy, declaring that the Veda was neither an inspired scripture nor free from error. He compiled an anthology of texts mainly from the *Upaniṣads*, the *Mahābhārata* and the *Manu-smṛti*, which under the name *Brahmodharma* became the official expression of the teachings of the Brahmo Samāj. Keshub Chandra Sen, the first non-brahmin to become *ācārya*, or presiding Minister, of the Brahmo Samāj, introduced some innovations which led to a split in the Brahmo community. He developed rituals to replace the Hindu *saṁskāras* (sacraments) and cultivated close connections with Christians. He also collected funds for victims of floods and famines, agitated against child marriage, and worked for the promotion of universal literacy. Early in his career he gave enthusiastic lectures on Jesus Christ, and therefore many took him to be a Christian. Later on, however, he began to consider himself a superhuman being and to expect worship by members of the Samāj. His 'New Dispensation' was to replace both the Old and New Testaments. A photograph shows him seated in the midst of a number of followers, each holding up a sign representing a different religious tradition. In consequence of his antics the Brahmo Samāj declined rapidly, and today it counts only a handful of members.

An unwilling patron saint of a Hindu missionary movement: Ramakrishna (1834–86)

It is an irony of history that one of the most active and outgoing movements of modern Hinduism carries the name of a man who lived a totally withdrawn life and did not want to hear of any 'charitable' activities or organizations. The man who became world famous as Ramakrishna Paramahaṁsa ('Supreme Swan', an expression of respect for highly venerated ascetics) was born Gadadhar Chatterji into a poor Brahmin family in the village of Kamarpukur in 1834. Already as a boy he displayed extraordinary psychic qualities, but showed no interest in academic studies. After his father's death his elder brother invited him to assist him in service at a newly built Kālī temple in Dakshineshwar, outside Calcutta.

When his brother died, he became chief priest. But he was no ordinary *pūjāri*, someone who just fulfils the obligatory requirements of worshipping the image at the prescribed times. He became an ardent devotee of the Goddess, fell into trance before her image, sang and danced ecstatically, so much so that his relatives considered him deranged. For almost twelve years he lived in a nearly continuous state of ecstasy. He threw away his sacred thread, making himself an outcaste, embracing untouchables and seeing God in everybody. He was interested in all religions. Just as he could see Kālī as Mother of the Universe, he also saw Jesus Christ bodily before him: he concluded that all religions lead to the same goal, being just different expressions of the same reality. As water is known by different words in different languages but is the same everywhere, so also the Supreme is the same, whether one called it Śiva, Viṣṇu, Allah or God.

He befriended Keshub Chandra Sen, at that time the leader of the Brahmo Samāj, and soon a growing number of visitors came to listen to his discourses. His main message was that the only actor in this world is God – humans are deluded in believing that they can do anything by their own power. All human sufferings and all problems arise from people's mistaken belief that they are agents. Ramakrishna discouraged his listeners from thinking that by doing good works they could improve the world. According to him the only important thing in life was to see God. Everything else followed from it.

The first modern Hindu monk: Vivekananda (1863–1903)

In 1883 Ramakrishna met a young man, Narendra Nath Dutt, who by the name Vivekananda would later found the worldwide organization of the Ramakrishna Mission. Narendra, born in 1863 into a pious and charitable family – his father used to read the Bible – was a brilliant student and initially an ardent member of the Brahmo Samāj. A friend persuaded him to come and meet Ramakrishna. Ramakrishna immediately recognized in him the incarnation of Nārāyaṇa, the Highest God, who had 'come to redeem humankind from suffering'. In a strange ritual – Ramakrishna placed his foot on Narendra's body – insight and the power to see God was communicated to him. Narendra now saw God everywhere and no longer took interest in anything else. When his father died, the young man had to take responsibility for his family. He encountered much difficulty in finding employment. His mother scolded him for his 'God-madness', exclaiming: 'If God is good, why are millions dying for want of food?' Narendra agreed and became an 'atheist'. However, falling exhausted on his bed after another frustrating day searching for employment, he had a vision: he saw how God's love and justice, providence and suffering each had its place in the world. From now on he knew that his true calling was to renounce the world and devote his life to the service of God. His only worldly concern was to see his mother provided for. He went to Dakshineshwar to pray to Kālī for money. Three times he tried, and three times he went into an ecstasy before her image, praying only for 'knowledge and devotion'. Like Ramakrishna, he realized that 'everything that is, is Mother'.

When Ramakrishna died in 1886, Vivekananda and a group of fellow disciples decided to establish an order of *saṁnyāsis* (monks) to continue to live according to the ideals that Ramakrishna had taught. In true *saṁnyāsi* fashion Vivekananda went on a year-long pilgrimage throughout the length and breadth of India. At Kanyā Kumārī, the southernmost tip, where the three oceans meet, he received his specific calling. Sitting at the Goddess temple, he reflected that instead of walking around and teaching the people metaphysics, *saṁnyāsis* in today's India should spread practical knowledge to help the masses improve their miserable condition. He remembered an often-heard saying of Ramakrishna's, that an empty stomach was not good for religion, and decided to do something about it. The idea of the Ramakrishna Mission as an agent of social uplift and practical education was born.

The Maharaja of Mysore asked Vivekananda to represent

Hinduism at the World Parliament of Religions that was planned in Chicago in 1893 for the fourth centenary of Columbus' discovery of America. The Maharaja covered all expenses and provided him with names and addresses of Hindus in Chicago who were prepared to offer him lodging. Vivekananda, arriving a month ahead of time, had lost the slip with the addresses, and quite literally had to spend the first night on the streets. Well-to-do theosophists whom he met by chance gave him accommodation until he established contact with the Hindu community.

After his first speech at the Parliament he was hailed as the most important delegate. He pleaded with his 'Brothers and Sisters of America' not to send Christian missionaries, but teachers and technical experts to India. He told them that it was an insult to a hungry person to teach her metaphysics, and an affront to starving people to offer them religion. Why did they not try to save bodies from starvation if they were interested in saving souls?

Vivekananda also reinterpreted Vedānta in a novel and exciting fashion. While all religions contain truth, Hinduism, in his opinion, will be the religion of the future, because it comprises all, possesses absolute tolerance, and has already reached its highest degree of perfection.

Vivekananda stayed in America for more than three years giving lectures, organizing aid missions for India, and establishing Vedānta societies in order to alleviate the spiritual poverty of the West. His ideal, as he presented it, was a combination of Indian religion and American science and management skills.

After landing in Colombo (Śrī Laṅka) on 15 January 1897, Vivekananda was triumphantly welcomed as a hero throughout India: he had given Hindus new pride in their tradition and shown himself the equal, if not the better, of Christian missionaries. In order to have a headquarters for his mission he founded the first Advaita Āśrama in Almora, in the Himalayan foothills. His 'practical Vedānta' was initially resisted by his fellow monks, who saw it as contrary to the purely spiritual teachings of Ramakrishna.

Vivekananda explained to them: 'See God in every man, every woman, every child. You cannot help them; you can only serve the One, who cares for them. Do it as a service to God. You must see God in the poor. The poor and the suffering exist for our salvation so that we can serve God, who appears in the guise of the beggar, the leper and the sinner.'

Vivekananda established two monasteries for training missionaries. In 1900, already mortally ill, he participated at the Paris meeting of the International Association for the History of Religions. Returning to India, he established *āśrams* and centres for relief work in Madras, Benares and Calcutta. In July 1902, aged forty, he died, probably of diabetes.

His foundation continued to grow, and is recognized today as one of the most active Hindu organizations. Besides maintaining *āśrams*, the Ramakrishna Mission manages many schools and hospitals, is active in publishing religious literature, is involved in relief work in areas where natural and man-made disasters have struck, and also continues the scholarly tradition initiated by Vivekananda. Its Ramakrishna Centre of Culture, built with the support of the Ford Foundation, is the venue for scholarly conferences and meetings, and offers accommodation to many foreign scholars as well. Vedānta societies in many countries have regular Sunday worship meetings, lectures and other activities.

Ramakrishna may have been averse to fame and organization; he might, nevertheless, have approved of what his disciple Vivekananda did in his name, and have been pleased at what the Ramakrishna Mission is accomplishing today.

A Hindu political saint: Mahatma Gandhi (1869–1948)

Many people in the West have seen the film *Gandhi*. It is not only a masterpiece of cinematography and acting but also an intense recreation of one of the most extraordinary lives of the last century. Gandhi was a Hindu. He considered himself a reformer of Hinduism and was shot by another Hindu, who believed that he had betrayed the cause of Hindus in their struggle with the Muslims.

Gandhi wrote an autobiography under the title *My Experiments with Truth*, recording his inner and outer development up to 1924. It is the best source for understanding him.

Mohandas Karamchand Gandhi was born in 1869 in Porbandar, Gujarat, into a family that had provided premiers for several small princely states. His mother was a devout Vaiṣṇava, who regularly visited the temple and kept religious fasts and observances. Gandhi grew up like most other boys in an Indian town. He did not excel in either academic studies or sports. When it was time to choose a career, he originally wanted to become a medical doctor. However, his Vaiṣṇava relations would not allow this: a Vaiṣṇava was not supposed to have anything to do with corpses or with cutting into the flesh of bodies – activities necessarily associated with modern Western medical studies. So Gandhi embarked on a career as a lawyer. It took courage for a young man with his background to study in England. Crossing the 'black seas' was associated with loss of caste, and, as he found out on the boat that took him to England, nobody could follow the English he had learned at school. It took him a long time and cost him a great deal of trouble to feel at ease in the foreign country. He eventually received his law degree, went back to India, lost his nerve during his first case in court – and did not know what to do after that.

In 1893 an assignment from an Indian firm with interests in South Africa brought him to the country where his decisive development from nondescript lawyer to highly profiled politician was to take place. For the first time in his life he experienced systemic racial discrimination. As a 'coolie lawyer' he was not accepted as equal by the white ruling class. The turning-point in his life came during a train journey from Durban to Pretoria. At one of the stations on the way, a white passenger entered the first-class compartment which Gandhi had occupied and demanded that the 'coloured' man move out. The conductor offered Gandhi accommodation in a second-class compartment. Gandhi refused to compromise. He would rather spend an uncomfortable night in a waiting-room than forgo his right to a first-class seat. He later stated that his 'active non-violence' – his most powerful political tool – dated from that moment.

Gandhi had always been religious. During his time in England he regularly attended church, and many friends suggested that he become a Christian. But Gandhi remained a Hindu. In South Africa too, he made the acquaintance of prominent Christians. One of them, C. F. Andrews, an Anglican minister, became his lifelong best friend and supporter, accompanying him back to India. When the South African government demanded that all Indians be registered and fingerprinted, Gandhi called for passive resistance. At that time he coined the term *satyāgraha*, 'truth-grasping', that was to shape his entire life. As he explained it, *satyāgraha* was the strength born of truth, love and non-violence. He would rather go to prison than obey an unjust law.

Gandhi's activities on behalf of the Indian community in South Africa made him a hero in India. He became widely known, and the fledgling Congress Party invited him to join their struggle for independence. One of the first things he did after returning to India for good in 1915, was to establish an ashram at Wardha, near Ahmedabad, in order to train suitable workers for the freedom movement. The rules were largely the age-old *yama-niyama*, the traditional Indian 'ten commandments' contained in the *Bhagavadgītā*. Two precepts were foremost and were considered the pillars of ashram life: *satya* and *ahiṁsā*, truth and non-violence. 'The first and foremost vow is that of Truth', say the *Ashram Observances in Action*. Gandhi was proud to have reversed the traditional formula 'God is Truth' into 'Truth is God'. Independent India was to be built on Truth alone. It chose as its motto for the state seal the Upaniṣadic proverb '*satyam eva jayate*: Truth alone will prevail'.

Throughout his life Gandhi called himself a seeker after truth. It had to be discovered in ever new situations. One of the preconditions for finding truth was self-effacement. Gandhi called it 'making oneself a zero' before the Infinite. His fasts and periodic withdrawals also served the search for truth. He called his entire campaign for independence and against any form of injustice *satyāgraha*, 'holding on to truth'.

The second, complementary vow was that of non-violence. For Gandhi it meant not only not killing, but active care and love extended to all living beings. *Ahimsā* (non-violence), too, became politically relevant. Over against the intentions of revolutionaries like Bal Gangadhar Tilak, Subhas Chandra Bose and Vir Savarkar, who wanted to drive out the British by revolutionary force, Gandhi insisted on a peaceful solution. When negotiations did not lead anywhere, he resorted to his 'weapon of truth'; non-cooperation and civil disobedience became the instruments through which freedom was won. On several occasions peaceful demonstrations degenerated into mob violence, and Gandhi had doubts whether his people was mature enough for *ahiṁsā*. He did penance to 'gain more credit from God' and always insisted that *ahiṁsā* had to be joined with fearlessness. He certainly gave a good example himself. He walked fearlessly into communal riots, faced British soldiers unarmed, did not interrupt his evening prayer services at Birla House even after death-threats had been made. He finally died there from the bullets of Nathuram Godse, with a 'He Rām!' (Oh Rāma!) on his lips.

Gandhi's achievements as one of the chief architects of India's independence are, of course, largely socio-political. He, however, saw himself throughout his life as a religious reformer, a reformer of Hinduism. He was a Hindu through and through, but he also criticized some of Hinduism's traditional failings. While convinced of the value of *varṇāśrama-dharma*, the caste-structure in its original form, all his life he fought against untouchability, which he considered an injustice and a blot on the face of Hinduism. He called the untouchables *Hari-jan*, 'People of God', and published a weekly by that name. For Gandhi, Hinduism was not simply identical with tradition, but had to be the religion of *satya* (truth) and *ahiṁsā* (non-violence), the lofty teachings of the *Bhagavadgītā* and the ideal condition of life as *Rāma-rājya*, the Kingdom of God.

MAHATMA GANDHI ON INDIA'S MISSION

I feel that India's mission is different from that of others. India is fitted for the religious supremacy of the world. There is no parallel in the world for the process of purification that this country has voluntarily undergone. India is less in need of steel weapons, it has fought with divine weapons; it can still do so.

I want to see God face to face. God, I know, is Truth. For me the only certain means of knowing God is non-violence – *ahiṁsā* – love. I live for India's freedom and would die for it, because it is part of Truth. Only a free India can worship the true God.

India has an unbroken tradition of non-violence from time immemorial. But at no time in her ancient history, as far as I know, has it had complete non-violence in action pervading the whole land. Nevertheless, it is my unshakeable belief that her destiny is to deliver the message of non-violence to mankind. It may take ages to come to fruition. But so far as I can judge, no other country will precede her in the fulfilment of that mission.

On India rests the burden of pointing the way for all the exploited races of the earth. She won't be able to bear that burden today if non-violence does not permeate her more than today.

Mahatma Gandhi, *Young India*

Gandhi, whom the Indian people called 'Mahātmā' (Great Soul), will also be remembered for his belief in women's moral and spiritual strength. Considering them an important part of the Independence Movement, he told women not to be 'dolls and objects of indulgence' any longer but to act as comrades at their husband's side. He further claimed: 'Man has regarded woman as his tool. She has learned to be his tool, and in the end found it easy and pleasurable to be such, because when one drags the other in his fall, the descent is easy.'

In 1925 Gandhi nominated Sarojini Naidu, a prominent female collaborator, as president for the Indian Congress. Six years later, due to women's active involvement in the civil disobedience campaign, Congress granted them political equality. Shortly before India gained independence, Gandhi said that he wished to see a young woman from a community considered 'untouchable' as the first President of Free India. While Gandhi may not be considered a feminist in the modern sense, he still helped women to emerge from their marginality and play a decisive role in the public sphere.

Ram Mohan Roy, Swami Vivekananda and Mahatma Gandhi all remained Hindus and tried to reform Hinduism from within. They appreciated some things which the West had done better than India and aimed to bring about a synthesis of Eastern and Western ideas. Their influence is still felt in India, although much criticism has been voiced against them as well.

Suggested further reading

Farquar, J. N. *Modern Religious Movements in India*. Oxford University Press: Oxford, 1914.

Parekh, M. C. *The Brahmo Samāj*. Oriental Christ House: Rajkot (Kathiawad), 1922.

Tendulkar, D. G. *Mahātmā*. 8 volumes, V. K. Jhaveri: Bombay, 1951–58.

Vivekananda, Swami. *Complete Works*. 8 vols. Advaita Ashrama: Calcutta, 1970–71.

14

Hinduism rejects the modern West

The movements connected with the names of Ram Mohan Roy, Swami Vivekananda and Mahatma Gandhi were open to influences from the modern West. They understood Hinduism as a developing, self-renewing and largely syncretic religion. Parallel to these there arose a countermovement that rejected everything foreign and insisted on going back to the roots. The ambiguity of those mutually exclusive trends has remained a fact of life in India. However, it is fair to say that, while India has in many ways become a modern country with big cities, an extensive railway system, airports, Hinduism overall has turned against westernization and modernization. Beginning with the nineteenth-century Ārya Samāj, the trend was continued by the early twentieth-century Hindū Mahāsabhā, the mid-twentieth-century Rashtrīya Swayamsevak Sangh, and the vigorous Shiv Sena and Vishwa Hindu Parishad of today. The Hinduism that has become a major political force in present-day India is not the religion of Ram Mohan Roy, Ramakrishna Paramahamsa or Mahatma Gandhi, but that of Dayananda Saraswati, Vir Savarkar, Pandit Mohan Malaviya and K.V. Hedgewar.

Dayananda Saraswati's Ārya-Samāj

Mula Shankara (1824–83), the later Swami Dayananda Saraswati, was born in Morvi (Gujarat) into a Śaivite Brahmin family. Keeping vigil on his father's orders during *Śiva-rātrī*, the highest

Worshippers entering temple gate, Vríndaban

feast of the Śaivites, he not only found his father soundly asleep before the *liṅga*, but also saw rats climbing up and down the image without the god interfering. That shook his faith in Śiva. The death of a sister and an uncle made him question the meaning of life. When he asked how to overcome death he was always told 'through Yoga'. He decided to become a *saṁnyāsi*. Against the wishes of his parents, who wanted to see him married, he left his home and wandered for fifteen years through India. He moved from one *guru* to the next without being satisfied by their answers to his questions. Finally he settled down in the ancient city of Mathurā, in today's Uttar Pradesh, with Virajananda Saraswati, a blind and temperamental, ultra-orthodox Hindu, who disciplined him severely. Before being accepted as disciple, he had to throw all his books into the Yamunā. After three years of humiliation and grammar study Virajananda dismissed his student, having renamed him Dayananda Saraswati, with the charge of 'teaching again in India the true *śāstras* (sacred doctrines), and to dispel the darkness which the wrong faith has borne'.

The 'wrong faith' was not only the foreign religion, Christianity, which had made inroads into Hindu India, but also everything that had been added to Hinduism since the original Vedas were proclaimed. So Dayananda told the *sādhus* (ascetics) in Hardwar that their *tīlakas* (signs on the forehead indicating membership of a particular religious sect) and ritual baths had no value, and he informed the Vaiṣṇava pilgrims that their holy book, the *Bhāgavatam*, was false and immoral. At first preaching only in Sanskrit, he began to attract large crowds by preaching in Hindī, the vernacular of much of North India. In 1873 he published the substance of his teachings under the title *Satyārtha prakāśa*, 'Light of Truth'. He claimed to present 'the original, eternal religion, the religion of humanity', attempting in the last two chapters to refute the teachings of Islam and Christianity. In fictionalized dialogues he debated with a missionary, and ended by 'proving' that the Bible was a book full of lies and immorality.

As far as Hinduism was concerned, Dayananda accepted only the original *Vedas* as the true Scripture, discarding the *Purāṇas* and other later literature that was the basis of the different *sampradāyas* (the traditional religious communities). He also rejected the usual form of worship of images in temples and re-introduced vedic fire sacrifice, the only ritual performed in Ārya Samāj centres.

Dayananda believed that he had a mission to lead India back to its original, pure vedic religion, and with that purpose he travelled around the country. In the Punjab he met with considerable success, and decided in 1877 to make Lahore the headquarters of his newly founded 'Association of the Āryans'. While the Ārya Samāj was originally resented by the orthodox for rejecting most of popular Hinduism, they welcomed it, because of its aggressive attitude towards Christian missions, as the 'Church militant of Hinduism'. Dayananda agitated against caste and child marriage. He proposed *śuddhi*, a purification ceremony for Muslims and Christians who wanted to revert to Hinduism, and he actively promoted Hindu missions in India and abroad.

In spite of his 'back to the roots' attitude, Dayananda claimed all achievements of modern science and technology – steam-engines, electricity, air-travel – as 'vedic': the Vedas, as the repositories of Truth, contain everything that later science is able to find. The Ārya Samāj is also 'modern' in its belief that salvation may be gained through social engagement. Its official creed proclaims, as the first goal of the Ārya Samāj, the improvement of the physical, social and spiritual conditions of humankind. It exhorts its members not to be satisfied with their own well-being but to consider everybody's well-being as part of their own.

After Dayananda's death the Ārya Samāj split into a 'conservative' and a 'progressive' wing. In 1886 the 'Progressives', under the leadership of Lala Hansraj, founded the Dayananda Anglo-Vedic College in Lahore, where modern education, including sport, was offered free of charge. The 'Conservatives' – also called the 'Mahātmā-party' – opened a *Gurukula*, a traditional vedic forest university, in Kangri, near Hardwar in the Himalayas. Children aged seven or eight entered the school for a sixteen-year training, during which they were not supposed to go home to their parents. All teaching was done in Sanskrit, and all subjects were traditionally vedic.

In later years the Ārya Samāj established numerous schools, as well as nursing homes and orphanages, in many cities and towns. It also began a 'Vedic mission' among the tribal peoples and outcastes. While the Ārya Samāj itself could claim success in many areas, its offshoots, founded by Ārya Samājists, were to shape India's public life even more decisively. In the Ārya Samāj Hindu tradition and nationalism, religious sentiment and practical engagement were successfully married: its offspring proved to be numerous and vigorous. Its conviction of the superiority of Indian civilization over that of the West has become fairly widely accepted in today's India, also by people who do not belong to the Ārya Samāj. In their estimation India's religion is far more profound than Western religion, and the best of Western philosophy does not come near the sophistication of Indian thought. They also think that the solutions which ancient India had to offer to social problems are preferable to Western ones, and as far as the sciences are concerned, that the West was ahead of India in the nineteenth century, but the principles upon which this progress was made were well known to the vedic Indians. And today, of course, Indian science and technology is second to none.

The first Hindu political party

In 1909, together with some other leading Ārya Samājists, Pandit Mohan Malaviya founded the Hindū Mahāsabhā, the Great Hindu Assembly, in order to give Hindus a political voice which, in his opinion, the Congress had denied them. The Mahāsabhā proclaimed 'Hindusthān', as the land of the Hindus, demanding for them the right to govern themselves according to Hindu laws. It was unable to prevent the Congress from becoming the official majority party, or the partition of India in 1947. But it continued to champion the Hindu cause and to agitate for Akhaṇḍ Bhārat, 'Undivided India', a reunification, if necessary by force, of India and Pakistan. It had its greatest theoretician in Vir Savarkar (1883–1966) who, in countless speeches and pamphlets, first exhorted Hindus to rise up and drive the British out of India, and then, after Independence, urged them to 'hinduize' India by overthrowing Nehru's 'secular' government and 'militarizing' Hinduism. His radicalism and his intemperate speeches earned him long periods of imprisonment under the British, and house arrest under the Congress. His essay on *'Hindūtva'*, in which he discussed what it meant to be a Hindu, became seminal. Savarkar distinguished *Hindu-dharma*, Hindu religion, which is divided into countless *saṁpradāyas*, or denominations, from *Hindūtva*, 'Hinduness', the common sociocultural substratum of Hindu India. The Mahāsabhā demanded that all Indian citizens accept India as their Holy Land, and that they abide by the Hindu ethos.

The Hindū Mahāsabhā, like all Hindu political organizations, contained a strong anti-Muslim sentiment that increased with the creation of Pakistan. Muslims in Bhārat ('Hindu India') who decided not to emigrate to Pakistan (which had declared itself a Muslim theocracy), became the target of Hindu suspicion and harassment. When, in the wake of the creation of East Pakistan – in effect the partition of Bengal – millions of Hindus fled to India, reporting forcible eviction from their homes and farms, and describing Muslim brutality and repression, the Jana Sangh, the 'People's Party of India', was formed with a strong pro-Hindu and anti-Muslim bias. One of its prominent founders was Shyamprasad Mookerjea, a former member of the Hindū Mahāsabhā and Minister for Industries and Supplies in Nehru's first Cabinet. Two other cabinet members – finance minister John Mathai and K. C. Neogy – also resigned and joined the new party.

Although the immediate occasion for the break was a disagreement with the ruling party, spokespersons for the Jana Sangh always maintained that it was 'not a disgruntled, dissident or discredited group of Congressmen' that founded the party, but that there was the deeper issue of an 'Indian' approach to things, which the Jana Sangh favoured. They feared that the Congress had become too westernized and that India might become a 'carbon-copy of the West'. In some states the Jana Sangh attracted a large following and became the target of attacks from both the Congress and the Left, who called the Jana Sangh 'fascist' and 'totalitarian'. It later merged with a number of other right-wing parties to form the Janata party, which came to power in 1977. It fell apart in the following year, largely due to internal differences over the role of the Rashtrīya Swayamsevak Sangh (RSS) which was prominently represented in the Janata party.

In 1980 a number of splinter groups from the former Jana Sangh and others formed Bhāratīya Jānata Party (BJP) which became the umbrella organization for Hindu right-wing political activism. Under the leadership of Lal Krishna Advani the BJP became an all-India nationalist movement, attracting worldwide attention through such media events as the *Rāma-śīlā-yātrā*, a public collection of bricks for the new Rāma temple to be built in Ayodhyā. It further made headlines through the *Ektā-yātrā*, 'unity pilgrimage', into the disputed Kashmir region, and finally through the 'spontaneous' upsurge of popular emotion that led to the destruction of the Babri Masjid in Ayodhyā in December 1992. This event was the spark that ignited the worst spate of Hindu-Muslim rioting since Independence.

The 'religious' theme that is currently being exploited by the Hindu political parties is the *Rāma-rājya*, the perfect rule of God on earth, portrayed in the *Rāmāyaṇa*. Gandhi had conceived the *Rāma-rājya* as the Kingdom of God, an India that followed highest moral standards and realized God's will. The *Rāma-rājya* of the BJP is less concerned with God's Kingdom and more interested in power and influence. The activists within the BJP either are, or were, members of the RSS.

Militant Hinduism: the *Rashtrīya Swayamsevak Sangh*

In 1925 K.V. Hedgewar, a medical doctor who never practised medicine, and a long-standing member of the Hindū Mahāsabhā, fearing the rising Muslim influence in the Indian National Congress, founded the *Rashtrīya Swayamsevak Sangh*, the 'National Volunteer Association' (RSS), which was to grow into the most powerful and controversial Hindu organization. Its weekly journal *The Organizer* is full of polemic and invective against all who do not share its philosophy. 'Organization' is the secret of its success: it is organized along paramilitary lines, with strict discipline, training camps and authoritarian leadership. All members have to attend regular indoctrination sessions and physical exercises, mostly with *lathis*, yard-long bamboo sticks, such as the Indian police use. The upper-echelon leaders are mostly unmarried and fully dedicated to the movement. By now there are thousands of *śakhas* (branches), all over India. The RSS claims a membership of five million. It declares itself to be a cultural organization, not a political party. However, many of its members have become involved in politics, and many of the leaders of the Hindu parties have an RSS background.

When K.V. Hedgewar died in 1973 he was succeeded by M. S. Golwalkar as *Sarsanghachalak*, Supreme Leader. Golwalkar, in his *Bunch of Thoughts*, openly laid out the ideology of the RSS. He declared Muslims, Christians and Communists enemies of India, and let everybody know that there would be no place for them in a Hindu India. He quite sincerely believed that the Hindu nation had a divine mandate to spiritualize the world and that the RSS was the instrument by which to realize it. Golwalkar's successors mitigated

THE MISSION OF THE RSS

It is clear, therefore, that the mission of reorganizing the Hindu People on the lines of their unique national genius, which the Sangh has taken up, is not only a great process of true national regeneration of Bharat, but also the inevitable precondition to realize the dream of world unity and human welfare. For, as we have seen, it is the grand world-unifying thought of Hindus alone that can supply the abiding basis for human brotherhood, that knowledge of the Inner Spirit which will charge the human mind with the sublime urge to toil for the happiness of mankind, while opening out full and free scope for every small life-specialty on the face of the earth to grow to its full stature.

This knowledge is in the safe custody of Hindus alone. It is a divine trust, we may say, given to the charge of Hindus by Destiny. And when a person possesses a treasure, a duty is laid upon him to safeguard it and make it available for the welfare of others. If he fails in that supreme duty he ruins not only himself, but also others. Hence the sacred duty of preserving the Hindu Society in sound condition has devolved on us.

M. S. Golwarkar, *Bunch of Thoughts*

the stance on citizenship in a Hindu *rāṣṭra* (a country dominated by Hindus) to include all 'who believe in the one-culture and one-nation theory'. They thus returned to Savarkar's notion of a *Hindūtva* that is cultural rather than religious. The involvement of the RSS in virtually all Hindu causes often makes it difficult, if not impossible, to discern whether the RSS, the Hindū Mahāsabhā, the BJP or the Vishwa Hindu Parishad are involved.

The Vishwa Hindu Parishad

The Vishwa Hindu Parishad, 'Hindu World Association' (VHP), was founded on Kṛṣṇa's birthday, 29/30 August in 1964, in

Bombay (since renamed Mumbai). The invitation to meet was sent out to some 150 religious leaders – some Sikhs were also among them – by Swami Chinmayananda, who had established a centre for the training of Hindu missionaries in Sandipani Sadhanalaya in a suburb of Bombay. Swami Chinmayananda became President, S. S. Apte (a prominent RSS member) the General Secretary; and M. S. Golwalkar, at that time the Sarsanghachalak of the RSS, was the most important person in the background. The Vishwa Hindu Parishad aspires to reawaken Hindu consciousness and to bringing about worldwide cooperation among Hindus. It also attempts to articulate a kind of universal Hinduism, to modernize Hindu tradition, and to give political power in India back to the Hindus. Its definition of 'Hindu' is fairly liberal and meant to include not only those that are born into Hinduism, but everyone, everywhere, who is willing to 'believe in, respect or follow the eternal values of life that have evolved in Bhārat'.

The first major public event organised by the VHP was a Hindu World Conference in Prayāg (Allahabad), coinciding with the Kumbhamela, a great meeting of all the religious orders, in January 1966. It was supposed to be the first such conference since that called by Emperor Harshavardhana in 648 CE. A further conference was held in Allahabad in 1979. The VHP met in Delhi in 1982 to determine its organizational structure. It now has its headquarters in a modern suburb of Delhi. Given the very ecumenical membership of the VHP, it is not surprising to see it supporting various, not always identical, goals. The core of the VHP is certainly formed by recognized traditional leaders, but the prominent presence of business and political leaders lends some extra dimensions to this movement. There is no doubt that the VHP, through its numerous initiatives and programmes worldwide, has become a major influence in Hinduism, especially among Hindus outside India. Ideologically conservative, even reactionary, in its practice it is modern and progressive.

Politically active Hinduism is a new phenomenon as far as more recent Hinduism is concerned. It links up historically, however, with pre-Muslim India, where Hinduism was not only the religion of Hindus, but also their form of government and their culture. Whether revivals on such a broad scale are possible remains to be seen. The attempt of Muslim mullahs in Iran to turn back the wheel of history and re-establish an essentially pre-modern society on the basis of religion can be called neither successful nor desirable. A Hindu India would certainly be a modern India. How it would look and how it would accomplish its aims as a *Rāmā-rājya*, is impossible to tell.

Suggested further reading

Ghose, S. *Modern Indian Political Thought*. Allied Publishers: New Delhi, 1984.

Golwalkar, M. S. *Bunch of Thoughts*. Vikrama Prakashan: Bangalore, 1966.

Jhangiani, M. A. *Jana Sangh and Swatantra: A Profile of the Rightist Parties in India*. Manaktalas: Bombay, 1967.

Rai, Lala Lajpat. *The Ārya Samāj*. Longmans: London, 1932.

Ferris wheel at folk festival

15
New faces of Hinduism

Most of ancient Hindu tradition is anonymous or attributed to legendary personalities, such as Vyāsa who is credited with having authored hundreds of different works. Those mediaeval personalities who became founders of distinct schools, like Śaṅkara or Rāmānuja, are perceived as recipients of a definite and final divine revelation for all of humanity. Their followers cannot but reject the teaching of the 'others' as not being the Truth. In the twentieth century a new type of 'pluralistic' *guru* has emerged: individuals, both men and women, who claim to be divine representatives, if not incarnations, but who also respect and tolerate others with a different message. Fairly tightly knit communities form around particular *gurus*, satisfied to receive God's message through them and not interested in fighting those who follow other teachers. Contrary to the teachers of old, who usually applied strict criteria of eligibility, contemporary *gurus* are usually liberal, admitting everyone to their fold regardless of caste, sex or nationality. Quite often they travel abroad and even have followings outside India. From the very large number of such new faces only a few will be chosen here – dozens more could easily be named.

Ramana Maharshi (1879–1950)

Venkataraman, who would later be called Ramana Maharshi, was born in 1879 at Tiruchuzhi in South India. After attending elementary school in his home town, he entered the American Mission High School in Madurai, a famous Hindu place of pilgrimage. When he was sixteen he had the strange experience of dying while fully awake. His limbs became rigid and his breathing had stopped, but his mind felt alive and conscious. He became experientially convinced that his true Self was spirit, not identical with the body. The experience itself lasted only about half an hour, but after it he lost all interest in his studies, his family and friends. His only concern was the spirit-self. Without informing anyone he left for Tiruvanammalai, the ancient sanctuary of Śiva represented in Aruṇācala, the 'Red Mountain', that dominates the town. There he settled in a dark, underground pit, engaging in silent meditation. So intense was his concentration that he did not notice the vermin that infested his body. Someone discovered him, unconscious, and nurtured him back to health. His extraordinary *tapas* (self-mortification) brought him attention. Local *sādhus* (ascetics) took care of him, and people started to visit him regularly. To avoid this unwanted publicity he moved out of town into a cave in Aruṇācala. When his identity became known his mother came and tried to persuade him to come home. He did not break his vow of silence but scribbled on a slip of paper: 'The ordainer controls the fate of souls in accordance with their past deeds: whatever is destined to happen will happen, do what you may to stop it.' In spite of his strict *mauna-sādhana* (vow of silence) people came and begged him to be their *guru*. He wrote brief answers to their questions on a slate or a piece of paper. His teaching remained the same throughout his life: 'Incessantly pursue the question Who am I? Thus you will come to know your true Self and thereby attain liberation.'

From 1907 onwards a growing circle of followers settled around him. While maintaining his austere lifestyle and periodically withdrawing into solitude, he was quite concerned for his fellow-humans, and visitors thought him welcoming. They received consolation in their grief, healing from their sicknesses, and above all they experienced peace of mind in his company. Ramana Maharshi's proverbial kindness also extended to animals: monkeys, dogs, cows roamed freely in the ashram grounds. In 1916 his mother joined him and became his disciple. She stayed with him up to her death in 1922, and her place of burial became a shrine as well as a place of pilgrimage.

For about thirty years Ramana, with a growing number of followers, lead a peaceful and withdrawn life. Important visitors came and went, books were written about him. Yet he remained the same, unaffected and unimpressed by his growing fame. In 1948 a small growth appeared on his left elbow. It was surgically removed but came back. It was diagnosed as malignant and amputation was recommended. Ramana Maharshi refused: 'The body itself is a disease,' he argued, 'let it have its natural end. Why mutilate it?' Still, various treatments were tried, several operations performed. He suffered greatly but stayed calm: 'We have to be witness to all that happens,' he said. While his bodily health rapidly declined, his mind remained clear to the very end. He died on 14 April 1950. People who witnessed his death were amazed by the extraordinary peace that radiated from him.

Ramana Maharshi did most of his teaching orally. Only a few small texts from his pen have become known. In all of them he taught the same: seek your true self! When visitors came, he would ask them: 'Who are you?' Not satisfied with their identifying themselves by their names, professions, place of birth, etc., he would press on: 'Who are you?' The true self has no name. He dismissed traditional philosophical debates about the nature of the Ultimate and the reality of the world as meaningless in the face of the all-important question: 'Who am I?' One of his Tamil poems succinctly summarizes his teachings:

> The world is real for the ignorant and for the wise; for the ignorant, reality is measured by the world, for the wise, reality is infinite and the foundation of the world.

> Both say 'I', speaking of the self, the ignorant and the one who knows; for the ignorant the 'I' is defined by the body, but the wise know that within the body the unlimited self shines with its own splendour.

Aurobindo Ghose (1872–1950)

In 1879, when he was seven, Aurobindo's parents sent him, together with his three brothers, to England in order to let him grow up as an Englishman rather than a Bengali. He proved a brilliant student, winning prizes in Latin, Greek, English and History at Cambridge. However, contrary to the wishes of his westernized father, he joined the Indian revolutionary student club 'Lotus and Dagger' and intensely studied European revolutionary movements.

Back in India, in 1893, he immediately became a member of the radical freedom movement. He did not believe in non-violence, and rejected Gandhi's approach. He gave a militant, nationalist twist to the *Bhagavadgītā*. For him nationalism was a religion through which God would be realized in the people: 'The 300 million people of this country are our God.' To reach that goal Aurobindo even got involved in terrorist activities. After one bomb attack he was arrested and sentenced to one year in jail. He was shattered. He had believed that he had God's protection while doing God's work. However, while in prison he had visions and heard voices. He began to see Kṛṣṇa everywhere and was told that his mission, after leaving prison, was to announce to the world the truth of the *sanātana dharma* (the eternal law) for whose sake India would be elevated above all other nations. Aurobindo now understood the truth of Hinduism in a manner in which he had not understood it before.

Warned that the British Government was about to deport him to the Seychelles, he fled to the tiny French colony of Pondichéry, about a hundred kilometers south of Madras, which he was never to leave again. Aurobindo saw his mission in preparing himself for the *śaktinipāta* (the descent of power), through which he would become the *avatāra* of the twentieth century. He withdrew to meditate and write. The ashram, which attracted more and more members and visitors, was managed by French-Egyptian Mirra Alfassa, the 'Mother', who controlled access to him.

Aurobindo started a journal, *The Ārya*, which he filled with his own thoughts and reflections. His idea of Hinduism was not a mere revival of old traditions, but a creative reinterpretation, that was stimulated by contemporary Western thought. In particular, Henri Bergson's philosophy of the life force fascinated him. In his *magnum opus*, *Life Divine*, he developed an evolutionary vision of humankind, culminating in the creation of a race of gnostic beings in which the evolution of the divine life on earth finds its fulfilment. Based on traditional Hindu notions, Aurobindo's thinking includes many other sources as well and soon attracted Westerners. His openness to all expressions of human creativity, his special concern for the improvement of women's education and his idea of a world-community eventually led to the foundation of Auroville, a futuristic city in the vicinity of Pondichéry, home to artists and academics, writers and meditators.

When Aurobindo died in 1950 he had not achieved *śakti nipāta*, the divine empowerment, and he had not proclaimed himself the *avatāra* for his age. However, his massive literary work, his 'Integral Yoga' and his community of followers are a legacy which has continued to provide inspiration and which has certainly shown that Hinduism need not be conservative and archaic, but can be a spiritual force for the present age.

Sarvepalli Radhakrishnan (1888–1975)

A younger contemporary of Aurobindo, Sarvepalli Radhakrishnan in his own way pursued the same goal: to rethink Hinduism in contemporary terms, open it up to the world and develop its potential for the whole of humankind.

Radhakrishnan grew up in Tirutani, a small South Indian pilgrimage town. He studied at Christian missionary schools, graduated from the well-known Madras Christian College, and had a distinguished academic career before mounting the political stage. In 1936 he was appointed Spalding Professor of Eastern Religions and Ethics at Oxford. Subsequently he held several important ambassadorial positions – among others as Indian ambassador to the United Nations and to Moscow – before he was chosen Vice-President, and then President of India (1968–73).

As a student he had been irritated by occasional remarks of his missionary teachers regarding the absence of an ethic in Hinduism. To prove them wrong he wrote an MA thesis on the 'Ethics of Vedānta'. As a young professor he went through the whole of India's philosophical tradition, producing a *History of Indian Philosophy* that also became very popular in the West. In many other books, and later in public speeches, he expanded on Hinduism as the 'Fundamental Religion of the Spirit'. According to him, Hinduism, while historically first realized in India, was in fact non-sectarian and universal. He tirelessly proclaimed the essentially spiritual nature of humans and admonished religious leaders to not reduce religion to tradition and ritual, but actively to engage in alleviating human misery and need. In politics he upheld high moral standards, perceiving his role as President of India as that of 'the conscience of the nation'. While philosophically an Advaitin, he did not restrict himself to expositions of the historic texts but re-thought the principles, trying to apply them to contemporary individual and social problems. Like Aurobindo, however, he did not reduce human nature to the empirical 'average' but believed in a higher destiny. If humans have evolved from lower forms of life to reach the present condition of *homo sapiens*, their development must not stop there. Humankind has to move higher and eventually reach a condition in which it becomes one with the deity. God is only seminally present in the world, and he has to be brought to fulfilment. He himself is involved in the suffering of humans, and this will come to an end only 'when God becomes the "all in all", when the solitary, limited God becomes the Pantheistic Absolute'.

A. C. Bhaktivedanta Swami (1896–1977)

Better known under his honorific, Prabhupāda', Bhaktivedanta Swami, the founder of ISKCON (International Society for Krishna Consciousness, popularly known as the Hare Krishna Movement), was probably the most successful propagator of Hinduism abroad. Born in 1896 as Abhay Charan De into a merchant family in Calcutta, he grew up in the vicinity of a Rādhā-Govinda temple, a place he loved to visit even as a young child. His father nurtured his devotion, but when Abhay was old enough to start schooling he refused to go to school and had to be taken there by force. Religious activities remained the most important part of his life even then.

When he was twenty he entered the Scottish Churches' College, a respectable Calcutta institution, run by ministers of the Church of Scotland. During his third year at college, he was married to a young girl of his father's choice. The next year he received his BA degree. The first thing he did was to fulfil a long-standing wish: a pilgrimage to Jagannath Puri, the famous temple-city on India's East coast. He became involved in Gandhi's independence movement, but had neither job nor income at that time. Eventually his father arranged an apprenticeship for him with his family doctor, who also ran a small pharmaceutical laboratory. For the next few decades Abhay produced and sold soaps, drugs and chemicals to earn a living for himself and his family, but his heart belonged to his religion.

In 1932 a decisive event took place: a friend asked him to meet 'a *sādhu* from Mayapur' (in West Bengal). Abhay did not have a very high opinion of *sādhus* and declined. But he allowed himself to be persuaded to meet Bhaktisiddhanta Saraswati Thakur, who was eventually to become his *guru*. While up to then the cause of India's independence and Gandhi's freedom movement were the chief concerns in his life, he let himself be convinced by Swami Bhaktisiddhanta that the preaching of Kṛṣṇa consciousness was a more urgent task, regardless of whatever political system happened to prevail.

Swami Bhaktisiddhanta was the head of the local Gauḍīya *maṭha* (monastery), which had been founded by his *guru* and father Bhaktivinoda Thakura. Bhaktivinoda had begun what became known as the Gauḍīya Vaiṣṇava Mission. He not only revived Caitaṇya's teachings but also urged his followers to go out and preach his message to the whole world. In 1932 Abhay moved his business to Allahabad, where he received initiation and became a formal disciple of Swami Bhaktisiddhanta. He tried to reconcile business, family life and preaching. His wife was not very co-operative and refused to join the *Bhagavadgītā* sessions at their home. His business also suffered. But his conviction grew that his real calling was in the spreading of Kṛṣṇa consciousness. His *guru* urged him to preach, write and print books for the cause of Kṛṣṇa. There also was a statement in his horoscope, made shortly after his birth, that at age seventy he would cross the ocean, become a great exponent of religion and establish 108 temples.

When Bhaktisiddhanta died late in 1936, quarrels broke out among his disciples about leadership and ownership of the *maṭha*. As a householder Abhay was not directly involved, but from now on he was religiously on his own. He moved back to Calcutta and began to publish a magazine, entitled *Back to Godhead*. He wrote most of the articles himself, financed and distributed it personally. He spent less and less time with his family and finally, after some disputes, he left his wife in order to devote himself fully to religion.

A League of Devotees, which he had established in the late forties in Jhansi, Uttar Pradesh, floundered and he found it difficult to survive, moving from place to place. He continued producing and distributing his magazine from Delhi. Finally he decided to settle in Vṛndāban, about eighty miles south of Delhi, in the holiest place for Gauḍīya Vaiṣṇavas, who had several major centres there. Finding accommodation in a temple building, he was persuaded to produce books, not just magazines. His fellow Vaiṣṇavas also urged him formally to accept *saṁnyāsa*, initiation into the monastic order, which they considered a precondition for effective preaching. The name he received was Abhay Caranaravinda Bhaktivedanta Swami. Noticing that few people were prepared to listen to him, he decided to write a book. In the time-honoured Indian tradition this would not be an independent statement of his own thinking but a commentary on an established text. What greater text for a follower of Caitaṇya than the *Bhāgavatam?* It is also a huge text. A. C. Bhaktivedanta planned not one but fifty volumes of text and interpretation, but did not have money to produce a single one! Somehow, by the grace of Kṛṣṇa, things came together.

Swami Bhaktivedanta found some money, a printer, paper (at that time paper in India was strictly rationed), and after moving back and forth between Vṛndāban and Delhi many times for proof-reading, fund-raising, persuading the printer to continue work, he had the first volume ready in 1962. He now set out to sell it and distribute it to prominent personalities. The response was encouraging, and so he embarked on writing the next volume, which appeared in 1964. The following year the third volume was ready.

Bhaktivedanta had not given up his dream, or rather, he had not forgotten the commission he had received from Bhaktisiddhanta Saraswati forty years earlier, to preach Kṛṣṇa religion in the West. He was sixty-nine now. Through a casual acquaintance he found a sponsor in the USA and after some arguing with Mrs Morarji, the owner of Scindia Steamship Company in Bombay, he received a free ticket on a freighter that took him to New York. He arrived after a journey of thirty-five days, during which he suffered two heart-attacks. He had no more than forty rupees and twenty dollars (which he had received for the sale of his three-volume set of the *Bhāgavatam* to the captain of the boat) and one hundred and ninety-nine sets of his work. After spending the first weeks with sponsors whom he had never met before, in Butler, New Jersey, he decided to move to New York. Since he was quite literally penniless and without an income he depended on casual acquaintances to put him up. He eventually settled into a seedy apartment in a run-down area of New York, trusting that by the grace of Kṛṣṇa, as whose servant he had come to the West, he would find disciples, establish a temple and disseminate Kṛṣṇa consciousness throughout the world.

It is amazing that this septuagenarian, with no life-experience in the West, let alone New York, with a heavy Indian accent and without material resources, should have started a movement that twelve years later quite literally spanned the whole world. On 14 November 1977 Swami Bhaktivedanta, affectionately called Prabhupāda ('The Lord's Feet') by his disciples, died peacefully, as he had desired, in Vṛndāban, India, content to have fulfilled his life's mission and his *guru*'s command. His disciples built a beautiful, elaborate *sāmadhi* (a chapel-like structure) over his place of burial, close to a large temple, a school and a guesthouse in their charge.

Śrī Krishnaprem Vairāgi (1898–1965)

Not long ago Hindus who travelled 'across the black waters' lost their caste, and foreigners, *mlecchas*, were, religiously speaking, outcastes. Since then it has become almost a requirement for Indian *gurus* with any standing to travel abroad and surround themselves with foreign disciples. Many new Hindu movements have opened their doors to all those willing to abide by their rules, and no longer discriminate against non-Indians. It is still rare, however, to find a foreigner accepted as a *guru* by native Hindus. Possibly the first of these was the man who became known as Krishnaprem.

Born Ronald Nixon in 1898 in Cheltenham, UK, he studied classics and science at Cambridge and served as a fighter-pilot in World War I. He later came into contact with the Theosophical Society. He felt attracted to Buddha and India, the Buddha's home country, and so took in 1921 the first opportunity that offered itself after his graduation to go as English teacher to India. Invited by Vice-Chancellor Cakravarti, a prominent theosophist, to Lucknow, while staying in the Cakravartis' guest-house he became a disciple of Monica Cakravarti, the Vice-Chancellor's wife, from whom he later received *dīkṣā* (initiation). In 1928 she retired to Almora and accepted *saṁnyāsa* from the hands of a Goswāmi from Vṛndāban (who acted as priest of the Kṛṣṇa shrine). Yashoda Ma, as she was henceforth known, then initiated Ronald Nixon, who assumed the name Krishnaprem. He began to lead the very austere life of a Vaiṣṇava *vairāgi* (renunciant). In the small ashram, which was completed in 1931, Yashoda Ma taught basic skills and hygiene to the nearby village children, while Krishnaprem was in charge of the library. He later took over as cook and temple priest as well.

Krishnaprem's friends admired him as a model *vairāgi*: he observed all regulations concerning food and worship and became fully accepted by Hindus as teacher and priest. He was, by then, fluent in Bengali and Hindī, studied Sanskrit and Pali, and wrote several works that were appreciated by scholars and seekers alike. After Yashoda Ma's death in 1944 he remained administrator of the ashram for over twenty years. He died in 1965. Hundreds of villagers, who had great affection for him, took turns in carrying his body to the burial grounds. He did not develop any new teachings of his own but was fully satisfied to imbibe and share traditional Kṛṣṇa religion. Once, during a train journey, he was confronted by an English lady who berated him for becoming a Hindu and 'throwing everything away', his religion, his culture and his country. When she asked 'What have you gained?' Krishnaprem, smiling, showed her his image of Kṛṣṇa and said: 'I have won Him, my Kṛṣṇa!'

Bābās and Mās

Affectionately called *bābā* (father) and *mā* (mother), many charismatic Hindu men and women who are not part of an older, acknowledged *Saṁpradāya*, and who have not been ordained into *saṁnyāsa* by the established authorities, have gathered followings both in India and abroad. Their teachings are very often idiosyncratic and they are sought out because of their extraordinary powers of healing or of insight. Their number in today's India is very large, and the three mentioned here do not exhaust the great variety of new faces under which contemporary Hinduism appears. Their background is as varied as their clientele: some have gone through a traditional religious training, others are ordinary people who have experienced visions or became aware of possessing unusual powers by accident. They often contradict religious clichés and refuse to be subsumed under traditional schools of thought.

Sāthya Sāī Bābā (1926–)

Born in 1926 in Puttharparthi, a small hamlet in the mountains of Andhra Pradesh, Sathya Narayan Raju, later Sāthya Sāī Bābā, announced at age fourteen that he was a reincarnation of the famous Sāi Bābā of Shirdi. The older Sāi Bābā, about whose identity hardly anything was known (some even thought he was a Muslim faqir) suddenly appeared in 1858 in Shirdi, Maharashtra, where he lived until 1918. He cured many villagers by applying the ashes of his holy fire to their bodies. Many miracles are reported to have been performed by him. He said that he would be reborn eight years after his death.

When Sathya Narayan Raju announced his new calling he left his family and began teaching the people who came to see him. A pious brahmin woman looked after him for several years until, in 1949, an ashram was built for him and his devotees. Prashanti Nilayam (Abode of Peace), some distance from Puttharparthi village, became the headquarters for all future activities. Those activities included the foundation of a number of ashrams in big cities, many of them large, modern edifices, schools, hostels, hospitals and all kinds of centres. Sāthya Sāi Bābā regularly visits all these places, and during his stay hundreds of thousands of people come to see him, touch him, and receive sacred ashes or other miraculously produced objects from him.

Meanwhile many Sāthya Sāī Centres have also been established outside India. A large literature has been produced, recording Sāthya Sāī Bābā's teachings, encounters with various people, his miracles and supernatural activities, which he also performs at a distance. Doctors and scientists have examined these and been convinced of their miraculous nature.

Sāthya Sāī Bābā is still alive; he claims to be the incarnation not only of the Sāī Bābā of Shirdi, but of Śiva and Śakti as well. He has prophesied that he will live for ninety-five years, after which time a third and final incarnation will appear. While much of what he says sounds like traditional Advaita Vedānta – he declares all ordinary perception to be illusion, all appropriation of body or things as belonging to the self as wrong – he also uses the words of the Christian gospels and invites all to lay their burdens on him. People with diverse religious backgrounds – or none – come to him, and Sāthya Sāī Bābā claims all the names of the Supreme used by them as his.

Ānandamayī Mā (1896–1983)

Everybody who knew her remembers her as a happy and cheerful girl. She was also a child who showed unusual feats of remembering past events. Nirmala Sundari, who would become known as Ānandamayī Mā all over India and beyond, was born in 1896 into a poor Vaiṣṇava family in Kheora, a small East Bengal village with a Muslim majority. Circumstances were not favourable for education. She received a total of about two years' schooling and did not read any books. Nor did she receive any formal religious education beyond the rituals performed at home. She learned to do *japa* (repeating names of God, or short formulae) from her devout father and participated in worship performed at home and in the temple. When she was twelve, her parents arranged a marriage with a man, later referred to only as 'Bolanatha', who was considerably older than her. It was to be a most unusual marriage. Apparently it was never consummated and Bolanatha, who had to move from place to place in search of employment, eventually became Nirmala's devoted disciple and servant. Before living with her future husband she moved in with the family of his elder brother and became very attached to her sister-in-law, who also later joined her as a disciple. Nirmala worked hard at household chores and did everything she was expected to do. After joining her husband, she spent many hours doing religious exercises and meditations.

One evening, without announcing it beforehand, she initiated herself. This was a most unorthodox thing to do. More unusual events were to follow. A year later she initiated her husband. From then on she lived almost exclusively for her religious calling. Many people came to see her, and often she went travelling to visit devotees. One of them gave her the name *Ānandamayī Mā*, 'Mother entirely made of bliss'. People considered her to be the incarnation of the Goddess. She herself refused to describe herself in any way other than by saying: 'I have always been the same, and I will always be the same. This body is illusion, and everything connected with it is just *līlā* (God's play).'

While not considering herself a *guru*, she nevertheless educated her followers ethically and spiritually. In her presence they felt calm and serene, but also aware of their personal shortcomings. Among her devotees were simple, uneducated people, as well as highly placed, academically trained persons. Kamala Nehru, the wife of Pandit Nehru, the Indian Prime Minister, was one of her early followers, regularly spending periods of time with her. Jawaharlal Nehru and his daughter Indira Gandhi, who also became a Prime Minister of India, kept up the contact. Gopinath Kaviraj, the most respected Hindu scholar of his time, was deeply impressed by her and called her *Ādya Śakti*, Primaeval Power. In 1982, when she was at a very advanced age, the assembled *sādhus* at the Hardwar Kumbhamela elected her their *Īśtā Devatā*, their chosen form of God to worship. Swami Shivananda, the founder of the Divine Life Society, called her 'the purest flower the soil of India has ever produced'.

Her life and actions remained a puzzle to outside observers. She could be most rational and compassionate, and she could also appear insensitive and whimsical. While hardly needing any food at all, when challenged she ate incredibly huge amounts. Friendly and sympathetic by nature, she could appear callous and even cruel at times. She would attribute these contradictions to the various needs of followers to realize God's transcendence and the world's transience. Health and sickness, wealth and poverty, life or death, in her view are only manifestations of the One, whom one has to find.

In 1950 an association was formed to take charge of the many ashrams and places that Ānandamayī Mā regularly visited. She travelled tirelessly from place to place, greeting and addressing ever larger crowds and chanting with them '*Satyam, jñānam, anantam, brahman*' (Truth/Reality, Knowledge, Infinity, Brahman). She considered it her life's mission to give witness to *brahman*.

Mā Jñānānanda (1931–)

Born in 1931, Mā Jñānānanda, 'Mother whose bliss is knowledge', is still alive and active. Renouncing her wealth and practising austerities, in 1975 she took *saṁnyāsa* from a well-known religious leader and soon became the focus of a large group of devotees. People from far and near come to Madras (recently renamed Cennai), where she now lives, besieging her with requests of all sorts: to secure a job, to find a suitable marriage partner, to regain health. She understands all these mundane concerns and people are convinced that she is offering help in all these needs, but her real message is to find God. Since she is a woman, women find it easier to approach her than men do. She is criticized by orthodox *gurus* for not complying with traditional Hindu rules for widows: Mā Jñānānanda does not wear the garb of a widow, does not shave her head, and does not lead a withdrawn life. But she apparently has the power to make people grow spiritually and to create faith in other people as well.

Many more Hindu philosophers and gurus could be mentioned – Hinduism has not ceased to bring forth most original personalities who not only keep the tradition alive but also transform it dynamically.

Suggested further reading

Aurobindo Ghose Birth Centenary Library. 30 vols. Shri Aurobindo Ashram: Pondicherry, 1972–5.

Gopal, S. *Radhakrishnan: A Biography*. Oxford University Press: New Delhi, 1989.

Osborne, Arthur. *Ramana Maharshi and the Path of Self-Knowledge*. Jaico: Bombay, 1962. *Satya Sai Speaks*. 6 volumes, Sri Sathya Sai Education and Publication Foundation: Kadugodi, 1974–5.

16

Hinduism and the challenges of today

As will have become clear so far, Hinduism has many faces and speaks in many voices, and one would not expect it to respond uniformly to the questions and challenges thrown up by the present. Many of the most revered and beloved contemporary Hindu saints hardly take notice of what others call the life-and-death issues of our time. Some of the *gurus* mentioned in the preceding chapter, while befriended by high-ranking politicians, business people, academics and other makers and shakers of the destiny of the world, completely ignore the day-to-day events about which the rest of the world gets excited and, when asked, have no comments to offer on issues that fill the pages of our newspapers. Their total detachment from the world and their single-minded focusing on the immaterial, eternal, spiritual Ultimate makes them unsuited as advisers on mundane matters. They take the view that all that happens has to happen and that the only worthwhile thing to do is the 'inner work' of ridding oneself of one's imperfections and preparing one's soul for the ultimate freedom which it desires by nature. The world, as they say, takes care of itself.

However, as we have also seen, there is a tradition in Hinduism that believes that humans have a responsibility to act and think, and that Hindu religious leaders have an obligation to help people lead good and fulfilled lives here on earth. The early vedic understanding of *dharma* implied that in return for following the rules of the law, one would enjoy prosperity in this life and happiness in the next. The considerable expense which kings and noblemen were prepared to incur in having public sacrifices performed would not make sense if they did not believe in tangible rewards. *Dharma* was also supposed to order society in an equitable way: it took care of widows and orphans, regulated the economy, gave everybody a place in society.

Similarly, while the God-intoxicated saints of the Indian Middle Ages taught otherworldly *bhakti* and were immersed in blissful devotion before the images of their God in the great temple centres, the countless pilgrims who every year retrace their steps usually hope for more tangible blessings: fine children, a good job, a salary rise, relief from sickness, a new home. They are quite open about it and are encouraged in their attitude by the literature put out by the pilgrimage centres, in which a great many stories of such 'successes' are told. As the large boards at the entrances of temples reveal, the priests operating from these also hope to gain more from worship than mere spiritual benefits. They have fairly concrete ideas about what their *pūjās* are worth in Indian rupees.

Over and above these mundane hopes that are fairly universally connected with the practice of religion, there is a more sophisticated, intellectual dimension to Hinduism, an attempt by philosophers and theologians to extrapolate from the principles of classical Hinduism answers to a range of vexing problems of private and social life. A minority of orthodox Hindus still strictly follow age-old rules with regard to hygiene, diet and social contacts. Yet the great majority finds itself in a quandary: beginning with schooling, through all kinds of employment, and by virtue of living in big cities with their public transportation systems, their large businesses, their open-for-all hotels and restaurants, most Hindus see themselves constantly compelled to violate ancient regulations concerning purity and propriety, and they have to live with it. Similarly, schools and newspapers, radio and television teach and broadcast a variety of views and opinions that challenge traditional doctrines and practices in vital areas.

The challenge is answered in manifold ways. An increasingly large number of Hindus turn the tables against the challengers. They accuse Western historians of misconstruing India's past, of suppressing the achievements of the ancient Indians, of neglecting India's contribution to world civilization. There is some truth in that charge. More detailed and more sympathetic research has resulted in a better appreciation of the real greatness of Ancient India, its material culture as well as its social structure and its administration. It has become acceptable to ask whether social arrangements, established over centuries in pre-modern India, might not be more suitable for today's Indians than arrangements introduced under Western colonial administrations. Similarly, architectural principles developed by indigenous builders could offer better solutions than those suggested by Western specialists, who operate in an entirely different climate. No doubt, a traditionally-built, thatched house in a village is not only cheaper than a concrete structure, but also more comfortable to live in. These are only small examples of a vast confrontation. The notions of the defenders of India's past greatness should not be brushed aside with clichés like 'Hindu chauvinism', 'Hindu fundamentalism' or 'Hindu arrogance'. While sometimes their rhetoric is overdone, there definitely is substance to their claims.

Another way of meeting the challenge is to accept modern Western methodologies and work out new solutions to existing problems. Thus the Western concept of equality before the law prompted Hindu reformers from the nineteenth century onwards to work towards mitigating, if not abolishing, the caste system, and to promote the equality of women and tribal peoples. Modern, Western-style education was also seen as a major tool to provide access for disadvantaged groups to social and economic improvements. No doubt, the introduction of modern industry has not had only negative effects, such as the disappearance of traditional handicrafts and home industries. It has also given many people from the lower strata of Hindu society a chance to earn comparatively high incomes and to emancipate themselves socially.

Increasingly, however, politically active Hindus desire to see 'Indian' solutions to Indian problems: they are convinced that Hindu social philosophy is superior to both socialism and capitalism, and that Hindu *dharma* alone can provide orientation and stability for Indian society. Such statements are not wholly unfounded. India's proverbial poor masses have not benefited visibly from either the socialist experiment under Nehru and his successors, or the capitalist liberalization that was initiated a few years ago. Unemployment and under-employment are endemic. The big cities, attracting the unemployed or under-employed rural population, cannot cope with the massive influx. Unrest and conflicts are rising, the crime rate is soaring. The educational system, while vastly expanded by comparison with earlier times, and possessing some world-class institutions at the top, is generally unsatisfactory. Apart from the traditional, family-centred transmission of values, which also shows signs of strain, there is no ethical consensus. Charges of corruption and unethical behaviour in public and private life abound. Self-respecting Hindus resent the imposition of a foreign system of values, and even bemoan the 'foreign-ness' of the Indian Constitution which was modelled after that of America.

Independent India under Jawaharlal Nehru chose to become a 'secular democracy'. Self-conscious Hindus were never happy with secularism and they still consider it 'un-Indian' and anti-Hindu. The Hindi equivalent of secularism (*dharmanirapekṣatā*) has connotations of an anti-religious and materialistic ideology. What it was intended to mean, however, was not disregard for religion and religious traditions, but a refusal to declare any one religion the state-religion (as Pakistan did) or the preferred religion. A whole generation of modern Indians now in leading positions in state and industry grew up as 'secularists'. However, not all of them were entirely comfortable with this. High government officials continued to consult religious leaders, and affluent business people made huge donations towards temple building and the upkeep of holy places. Recently it has become quite acceptable, even for Indians not committed to political Hinduism, to speak out against secularism. T. N. Madan, Director of the Institute of Economic Growth at the University of Delhi, a highly visible and widely respected public figure, called secularism 'the dream of a minority which wants to shape the majority in its own image' but lacks the power to do so. The 'minority' are westernized, largely uprooted bureaucrats and professionals. The majority of Indians, Madan holds, are still guided by their religious traditions and show no sign of abandoning them. Madan also cautions that a transfer of European secularism to India would not work, because the presuppositions are different.

This is the point for Hindus who want a Hindu state to replace the present secular democracy of India. Recently an all-India association of Hindu religious came out with a manifesto initiating a People's Consciousness Movement. They accuse the secular governments of having passed 'laws against *dharma*' and blame the Constitution for 'destroying the very roots of our country's cultural, religious and spiritual life'. They demand the use of the Indian name 'Bhārata' in English documents, and the replacement of the present national anthem (originally composed to greet King George V on his state visit to India) by Bankim Chatterjee's *Bande Mātāram*. In addition they also would require from all Indian citizens 'a declaration of patriotism'. Among their demands is also the 'eradication of the memorials of predatory, cruel and despotic rulers from the Mughal time'. The destruction of the mosque built by Babur over the ruins of the Rāma temple in Ayodhyā was part of this agenda. Similarly the 'liberation' of the Golden Temple in Vārāṇasī and the Kṛṣṇa *janma-bhūmī* in Mathurā are envisioned. British laws enacted between 1860 and 1935 ought to be thrown out and replaced by regulations 'based on the rule of *dharma*'. These Hindu traditionalists conclude their appeal by stating: 'After the rule of *dharma* has been established, there will no longer be famine, poverty, ignorance, unemployment. The unity and integrity of the country will be safeguarded. Corruption, immorality, lawlessness and insecurity will be eradicated.'

It has been a long time since Hindus had the opportunity to shape public life in India. For many centuries Hinduism was represented by *sādhus* with other-worldly interests and perceived, by Radhakrishnan in his time, as 'the religion of the spirit' without any political ambitions. Things have changed. Notwithstanding old monastic codes that prohibit the involvement of *sādhus* in worldly affairs, a large number of them today are involved in politics at all levels. There are at least a dozen now sitting in the *Lok Sabhā*, the Indian Lower House in Delhi, and many more represent Hindu parties at state and municipal levels. They defend their break with the rules of the past by saying that times are so desperate that the involvement for the sake of the *dharma* is required. Not all Hindus agree.

For the majority of Hindus the most important function of their religion is still care of the spirit: rituals to sanctify their lives, worship in temples to have a glimpse of the image of God, *satsaṅg* (congregational singing) with *gurus* to receive spiritual nourishment, pilgrimage to holy places to experience the sacred. As we have seen in the few examples of Hindu saints of more recent times, in spite of their solicitude for the poor, the sick, the disadvantaged, their real interest is and remains the spirit: God and the soul. Their own practice as well as their teachings focus on *sādhanas*, means to reach God, to find inner peace. These *sādhanas* are not very different today from what we know from former times: self-restraint, discipline, overcoming of anger, greed and delusion, worship, kindness, benevolence, chastity, repetition of sacred names or *mantras*, fasting and meditation. The paraphernalia may have changed slightly, the message is largely the same. In this sense Hinduism is still the *sanātana dharma*, the eternal, unchanging, universal religion, that teaches people how to lead a life that prepares them for the encounter with the Ultimate.

Much of Hinduism is homey, simple, traditional, but there is also a dimension that is sophisticated, profound and creative. This is *jñāna*, 'wisdom-knowledge', which has been prized as the highest achievement by Hindus and is also recognized by Western seekers as the most precious jewel in the crown of Hinduism.

The Nobel prize-winning physicist Erwin Schrödinger wished to see 'some blood transfusion from the East to the West' to save Western science from spiritual anaemia. He explicitly affirmed his conviction that Vedantic *jñāna* represented the only true view of reality – a view for which he was prepared even to offer empirical proof.

Aldous Huxley, whose *Perennial Philosophy* is not only an unsurpassed anthology of world religions but also an outline for a universal religion, similarly suggested that Vedāntic *jñāna* was the key to unlock the gate to the meaning of human existence. Summing up the wisdom of sages in East and West, he came to the conclusion that 'this teaching is expressed most succinctly in the Sanskrit formula *tat tvam asi* ... and the last end of every human being is to discover the fact for himself, to find out who he really is'.

The Hindu notion of *jñāna* ('wisdom', 'in-depth knowledge', 'intuitive and direct understanding') provides an alternative to present-day approaches that is neither 'irrational', nor simply another variety of instrumental reason. It is a depth-dimension of 'reason' in which the theoretical and the practical join, free from many of the shortcomings of Western Enlightenment rationalism, such as its antireligious animus.

Jñāna allows us to re-connect rationality with reality, overcoming the truncated rationality of the modern West, which bracketed out the source and end of all human thought. An appeal to *jñāna* is not an appeal to right-wing politics, obscurantism, oppression and intellectual dishonesty. It is an appeal to the humane in thought and deed, to the integrity of thought and life, the continuity of consciousness and reality. While it contains elements of both 'faith' and 'science' as understood in the Western tradition, it is different from both and overarches them.

For the average person *jñāna* will appear in the form of *jijñāsa* – a reaching out to understand, rather than the possession of definite 'wisdom'. The existential nature of *jñāna* forbids its expression in dogmas and formulae. Although such formulae have been attempted – e.g. the Advaitic *brahma satyam jagat mithyā* ('brahman alone is real – the world is false') – the Advaitic understanding of *jñāna* is not necessarily the only one, and the formula can be interpreted in many different ways. *Jijñāsa* as the constantly renewed attempt to reach *jñāna* – a search informed by some inkling, a spark of illumination, some kind of spiritual gravity – is the response to new challenges and questions from the level of *jñāna*.

The exemplary character of *jñāna* consists in its synthesis of objective and subjective knowledge, its refusal to divide the world into fact and value, its insistence on rationality as reality which does not exclude anything. It combines insight into nature with reflection, objective knowledge with self-cognition. It implies and demands an ethic, a discipline as an antecedent to its application. By seeing *ātma-jñāna* (Self-knowledge) as irrevocably linked to *brahma-jñāna* (Knowledge of the Ultimate), and both as the deep foundation of any type of knowledge, it infuses into the human drive towards knowing the dimension of the *unum necessarium*, the one thing needed to save ourselves and the world in which we live.

Jñāna considers the 'ethic' of a person as the indispensable condition for 'knowledge'. The claim to be on the way to truth – *brahmajijñāsa* – can only be made after certain qualities of character have been established – freedom from passion, from egotism, from ambition – otherwise it is sheer hypocrisy. *Jñāna* would also expose the fallacy of a 'value-free' science: knowledge is a value by and in itself, and the search for truth is a value orientation. If it is not, it is a perversion. *Jñāna* could not be used to support the machinations of a criminal government, which science can do very well, as we all know.

Brahmajijñāsa as an effort towards 'meaningful knowledge', a search for reality and an ethical orientation can be real only in living persons, not in formulae or institutions. *Brahma-jijñāsa* is not an excuse to withdraw from the real-life concerns of one's time. Quite the contrary. It implies engagement at a much deeper level, and with a much greater stake in the outcome. There was practical wisdom in the traditional Hindu provision that only a person who had fulfilled all the usual obligations towards family and society was entitled to enter upon *brahmajijñāsa*. While the inner and outer independence of the *vānapraṣṭha* and the *saṁnyāsi* was essential, the search itself was seen as of utmost importance for family and society. Such mature seekers based their search on concrete knowledge and experience of 'real life'. They did not become 'other-worldly' in the wrong sense, i.e. they did not imagine a parallel world without the problems of this world, but plumbed the ultimate dimension of the world we all know or believe we know.

Suggested further reading

Chaterjea, P. C. *Secular Values for Secular India*. Lala Chaterjee: New Delhi, 1986.

Dumont, Louis. *Religion, Politics and History in India*. Mouton: The Hague, 1970.

George, A. *Social ferment in India*. Athlone Press: London, 1986.

Moddie, A. D. *The Brahmanical Culture and Modernity*. Asia: Bombay, 1986.

Index